PICTURING THE PAST

THROUGH THE EYES OF RECONSTRUCTION ARTISTS

Brian Davison

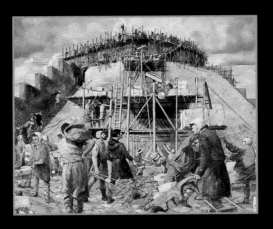

ENGLISH HERITAGE
GATEKEEPER SERIES

CADW

THE ART OF RECONSTRUCTION

This book looks at the way we picture the past. Four thousand years of history are in these pages, seen through the eyes of 27 different artists. Each has sought to recreate a place or an event as it may once have been.

Our most vivid mental pictures of the past often derive from historical epics seen on film or television. 'Living' reconstructions of this sort have enormous impact. By following a believable storyline they help us understand the actions and motivations of our ancestors, giving us a key with which to unlock the real past. We need to be on our guard, however: a compelling performance by a charismatic actor may result in continued screening long after historical research has cast doubt on the authenticity of the action, costumes or settings.

Whatever medium is used, no reconstruction of the past can do more than illustrate the state of knowledge on the day when it was created. The artists' reconstructions collected here were commissioned by English Heritage and Cadw, organisations which protect and care for our ancient sites and ruined buildings. The drawings were made for a variety of purposes: films, exhibitions, guidebooks and site information panels. All have the same object: to put flesh on the bare bones of the past by restoring – on paper, at least – what time has taken away.

Drawn reconstructions are one of the main ways in which we develop our ideas about the past. Each is the result of a prolonged and detailed collaboration: artists, historians, archaeologists, anthropologists and ecologists have each contributed from their own specialist knowledge. In the last resort, however, the success of that collaboration depends on the skill of

the artists. Some have deliberately limited themselves to architectural reconstruction, drawing on evidence from similar buildings elsewhere to paint in the missing parts or using their skills to 'cut away' exterior walls to reveal what might have gone on inside. Others have portrayed the people who built and used the buildings. Others again have depicted the most difficult subject of all: the long-lost ceremonies and rituals which once bound society together.

Behind this there lies an on-going debate among those who commission such work. Just how far we should go in trying to 'reconstruct' the past? Indeed, should we do it at all? Do we really have any right to influence how other people interpret their past? How certain of our facts do we need to be? If we have only 80% of the information necessary to reconstruct a place or an event, should we leave it there or make a guess at the other 20% in order to round-off the scene and make it work? Which is more important: the avoidance of all invention or a drawing that makes visual sense?

This book responds to a remark made by a visitor to Stonehenge who, when told of the difficulties of being really certain about anything so old, said: 'I didn't come all this way to hear you say you don't know. I came to hear you make the best guess you can!'

Reconstruction drawing involves making the best guess we can. It does not set out to provide a once-and-for-all 'authoritative' view of the past. It aims to inform, but also to provoke. Is this what the past was like? If not, what was it like? Most importantly, how could we find out enough to settle the matter?

MAIN PICTURE *Neolithic engineering – one of the great timber structures built at Durrington Walls in Wiltshire. Buildings like these may have been the prototypes for the later stone structures at nearby Stonehenge (Peter Dunn)*

Copyright © 1997 English Heritage

First published in Great Britain 1997
by English Heritage, 23 Savile Row, London W1X 1AB
Edited by Ken Osborne · Designed by Martin Atcherley
Printed in the European Community

A CIP catalogue record of this book is available from
the British Library

ISBN 1-85034-593-5

FRONT COVER ILLUSTRATIONS *Top left: The Sanctuary
near Avebury seen in its final phase; top right: Robert
Dudley welcomes Elizabeth I to Kenilworth Castle in
1575; bottom left: Wroxeter Roman City, street scene
outside the market hall; bottom right: A Saxon
housecarl faces the Normans at the battle of Hastings*

TITLE PAGE *Construction work at Totnes Castle
(Ivan Lapper)*

THIS PAGE *An impression of the market place in the
small Roman town of Letocetum in Staffordshire in
the 2nd century AD (Ivan Lapper)*

CONTENTS

MINING FOR FLINT

Very little has come down to us from our remote past. This is hardly surprising. In the thousands of years since the Stone Age, whole landscapes have changed. We have removed forests and reclaimed wetlands, ploughed and farmed the land, built towns and cities. In many places we are now quarrying away the very structure of our land.

Only the most durable of materials can withstand such changes: organic materials like wood, bone, leather, basketry and cloth usually rot. Of all things, the longest lasting are stone and flint.

Long separated from their original wooden hafts and leather strappings, tools and weapons of stone or flint fill the display cases of our museums to illustrate the skills of our early ancestors. Sadly, most of the things which made their lives comfortable and enjoyable have crumbled and returned to dust. Only their spear-points, arrowheads, axes and scrapers remain to be found by archaeologists or turned up by the plough.

It is all too easy to be fascinated by the detail of these fine implements. Shaping stone was not an end in itself, however: it was a necessary part of making hunting weapons and tools, an activity which was itself an unavoidable preliminary to the serious business of finding the next meal! We may have found the missile heads but beyond this we cannot go. We can only guess at the skills and experience of the hunters, the camouflage and decoys that they used, yet these must have been even more important than the shape of the spear points.

This is where the imagination must take over if we are to recreate a world in which it could be necessary to spend an hour or so making stone spearpoints before going out to look for lunch. The appearance of the hunters, their skin and hair colour, their clothing, the presence or absence of dogs, the habitats of the animals and birds they pursued – these must all be evoked by the artist in order to complete a world which is understandable and credible.

Not everyone in that world was a hunter, of course, but everyone had to make a living. Five thousand years ago, in the period archaeologists call

ABOVE *At Grimes Graves in Norfolk the modern landscape is pitted with the traces of prehistoric flint mines. This was once an early industrial landscape, used by generations of miners. In the bottom of the mines, low galleries radiated outwards from deep central shafts to follow the best seams of flint. The timber staging platforms in Terry Ball's drawing are based on postholes found during excavation*

BELOW *When the main shafts were investigated by archaeologists neat piles of mining tools were found as well as a chalk figurine. These suggest that rituals may have been performed to ensure the continuing fecundity of the earth, as shown here in Peter Dunn's drawing*

ABOVE *The flint was extracted in galleries dug entirely within the thickness of the seams using tools made from deer antlers, bone and wood. Some air must have circulated in the galleries but the working conditions must have been cramped and stifling. The only light came from oil lamps fashioned in clay or cut from chalk (Peter Dunn)*

the Neolithic or New Stone Age, most people were farmers, combining tillage with stock rearing, basic forestry and land drainage. Some, however, were miners.

Away from the western uplands where hard volcanic rocks outcropped on the moorland hill tops, the only material suitable for sharp-edged tools and weapons was flint. This had to be won from the ground, for although flint pebbles could be found along river banks, really good quality flint lay deep in the chalk.

Extracting large nodules of flint in low galleries, using pick-axes and rakes made out of deer antlers and shovels made out of wood or bone, in the flickering light of oil lamps, must have been hard, sweaty and dangerous – a job for specialists. How this industry was organised we can only guess. It may have been a full time job, or seasonal work by men engaged at other times in farming, fishing or hunting. We do not know whether women were involved in any way. Whatever apparatus of ladders, platforms and haulage gear was used, it has left no trace in the debris-filled mine shafts. Only the miners' hand-tools survive, abandoned in the radiating galleries or carefully piled into tidy heaps at the bottoms of the main shafts where they have been found by archaeologists five thousand years later.

A major part of the output of the flint mines was axe heads. Good axes were vital in a countryside still half forested: axes to clear the land and shape ploughs, axes to square timbers for houses, axes to cut fuel for cooking and heating. Early farming practices required the regular clearing of forest land and as the population rose some management of the forest resource became essential. In the wetlands of Somerset, where early timber track-ways have been found, the materials used show a keen appreciation of the characteristics of different types of wood. Large numbers of narrow poles show that pollarding was common, with trees felled and encouraged to produce secondary growth which could be harvested at regular intervals. Heavy squared timbers reveal the remarkable carpentry skills of these early farmers with their flint axes and chisels.

The fertility of the earth in the replenishment of woodland must have been evident enough. However, the earth's ability or willingness to provide new seams of flint, and the chances of winning that flint in safety, must have seemed less certain. The association of piles of miners' tools with small rotund figurines of women, carved in chalk, suggests that the earth may have been seen as a being who could provide or withhold the basic material on which tool production depended. This sort of personification of the earth would open the way to other ceremonies of placation or appeasement, with rituals in the open air in newly-ploughed fields and clear-felled woodland as well as in the claustrophobic bottoms of exhausted mine shafts.

NEOLITHIC RITUAL

Ceremonies and rituals present the greatest challenge to the archaeological artist. From the evidence left behind by early farmers we can usually find out what they did and roughly when they did it. Sometimes we can determine how it happened. It is extremely difficult, however, to be sure of the motives behind their actions.

Imagine a Britain four thousand years from now. Civilisation has disappeared. Foreign archaeologists investigating a ruined church would note that it stood in an open space full of graves. Inside they would note more graves under the paving and the remains of memorial inscriptions on the walls. They might reasonably conclude that this was a tomb. They might speculate about the nature of the funeral ceremonies – but would they guess at weddings and christenings? What could they hope to know about the form of service used on Sundays or the carols that were sung at Christmas? Unless they came across a Bible or some hymn-books they might even find it difficult to be sure which god was worshipped in that place.

So it is when we try to imagine what went on in the ritual places of the past. We know what weapons people carried and what ornaments they wore, but we don't know how they may have painted and dressed themselves for different ceremonies; we don't know precisely where they stood or what gestures they made; we can't hear their songs and chants. All too often stone circles, burial chambers and the occasional imprint of a long-vanished wooden building are all we have in the way of evidence for the ceremonies which may have been fundamental to the life of early communities. The crucial importance of those ceremonies is indicated by the grouping together of precincts, processional avenues and tombs to form huge landscapes of ritual: landscapes made sacrosanct by the nature of the individual monuments. Some of these landscapes remained relevant to their communities for a thousand years or more. Across such a spread of time monuments were built, modified and eventually allowed to fall into disuse – but never were they forgotten.

By reading descriptions made by modern travellers and explorers we can get some idea of the rich ideologies which often characterise primitive communities. From anthropologists' films we can glimpse the complexity of their ceremonies. Without such information from recent times the archaeologist would be left groping for an explanation of the great ritual monuments of the remote past.

The precise meaning of what went on inside these great prehistoric structures will never be known. It is probable, however, that the ceremonies held there were intended to benefit the living as much as the dead. Whatever the immediate circumstances – birth, marriage, death or propitiation – the real purpose may have been to bind the members of the community together more closely through the observance of remembered rituals. Reference to nearby disused monuments built by ancestors and the recitation of a shared history (whether mythical or real) may have served to emphasise long-term continuity and ease the transfer of power and authority at times of stress.

LEFT *The modern village of Avebury in Wiltshire lies at the centre of a huge complex of prehistoric ceremonial monuments built over several centuries at the end of the Neolithic period. Here a harvest festival is shown taking place within one of the stone circles within the Great Henge. Judith Dobie has deliberately shown the people involved in a stylised way to emphasise how little we really know about them*

RIGHT *The most enigmatic of all the Avebury monuments is Silbury Hill, the highest man-made mound in Europe. It has been investigated several times without yielding any clue as to its purpose. Judith Dobie here shows the mound under construction in order to reveal its original stepped form. Again, the people are shown in a stylised way, stripped to the waist for working in the warm period after the summer harvest*

ABOVE *A mile from Avebury, on Overton Hill, there stood a wooden shrine (The Sanctuary). Much older than the Great Henge and Stone Circle, it was eventually linked to them by an avenue of standing stones. This could have been a processional way, as Judith Dobie has suggested here; alternatively, it may have been a taboo-road along which ancestral spirits walked from the old shrine to witness ceremonies within the henge*

EARLY SETTLEMENTS AND FARMING

The great ritual monuments of the prehistoric period bear witness to the religious and social life of long-settled societies. Only a well organised and economically secure community could make available the sort of labour force necessary to build great monuments like Avebury, Maes Howe or New Grange. The skills employed in their construction must have been developed, generation after generation, through the everyday work of forestry, field clearance, stone hauling and house building.

We now know something of the world of those farmers who first laid out our countryside as a patchwork of woodlands, fields and trackways. The story has not always been one of advancement. The making of barren moorland through a fatal combination of over-farming and a deteriorating climate is not just a modern phenomenon. The open heather-clad landscapes of Dartmoor or the Yorkshire moors may seem natural wildernesses: in reality they are ancient man-made wastelands.

Six thousand years ago, early pioneers attacked the forests which covered Britain at that time. They did it on a piecemeal basis, carving out small fields around their settlements and moving on when the soil was worked out. By about 2000 BC, however, some well-established communities were breaking in huge tracts of land and laying them out to form regular fieldscapes covering several square miles apiece. Such community enterprises speak not only of a remarkable degree of social organisation, but also of rising populations and competition for resources – the most crucial resource of all being land.

Depicting these early prehistoric landscapes is no easy task, if only because of the great range of subject matter: the size and shape of the fields, the nature of their boundaries, indications of climate, the location and appearance of buildings, the particular breeds of animals, the types of crop that were grown, even the natural background of birds and wildflowers. All evidence of this must come from the ground. Careful investigation of individual sites can produce cereal grains, flower pollen, and the dismembered skeletons of animals which were husbanded, hunted or trapped. A drawing of an ancient landscape may incorporate archaeological evidence painstakingly gathered from a number of sites over several decades.

Within these new farming landscapes the settlements seem to have been fairly widely scattered. A group of up to half-a-dozen buildings inhabited by an extended family of around thirty people seems to have been the norm. In western areas their houses and barns may survive as low tumbled stone walls: further east, in areas without building stone, only the imprint of their buildings may survive in the form of empty post sockets cut into the ground. The form of the roof structure, the roof covering, any external or internal plastering, or decorative colouring – all these are matters for informed speculation which is then given life by the archaeological artist.

LEFT *Carefully laid-out prehistoric fields were first noticed by archaeologists in the deserted uplands of Western Britain, but gradually their traces are being recognised under layer upon layer of later landscapes in the still-populated lowlands. Rising populations clearly brought competition for resources and a concern for agreed boundaries and a framework for daily living (Judith Dobie)*

RIGHT *The tombs and temples of early prehistoric people have always been easier to find than their homes. Wooden or mud-walled houses leave little trace above ground, and sometimes even the sockets for the posts have been ploughed away by more recent farmers. Here, the roof of a Bronze Age house found on Brean Down in Somerset is shown partly removed to reveal the interior (Peter Dunn)*

BELOW *The early Bronze Age saw a growing desire for prestige goods as a means of marking personal status. The more successful members of society used (and were buried with) finely-decorated beakers, axe-hammers of imported stone, and copper axes, daggers and gold ornaments from Ireland. Such conspicuous consumption ended with the change in funerary rite from burial to cremation (Judith Dobie)*

THE GREAT MONUMENT BUILDERS

The period around 2500 BC seems to have been an age of social and political change, at least in southern Britain. It is not clear whether this resulted from an influx of new settlers with different ways of life or merely from internal shifts within British society. What the archaeologist detects from a study of burial customs is an increased emphasis on individual status and the trappings of personal power. While the monuments themselves become increasingly elaborate, their smaller size and a move from enclosure to exclusion suggests they were built to stage ceremonies conducted for elite groups rather than for the community as a whole.

Where only the empty sockets of a once-imposing wooden building survive in the soil, it is difficult to be certain of its precise use. Archaeologists still argue about the use of the two large and elaborate timber buildings, the sockets of which were found at Durrington Walls in Wiltshire. Were these just larger-than-usual houses, or were they perhaps ceremonial buildings? Big round timber buildings seem to have become

RIGHT *Within the great encircling ditch and bank of Durrington Walls in Wiltshire archaeological excavation revealed traces of two circular wooden structures. From the size and depth of the sockets we can work out how big the posts must have been. Peter Dunn's drawing of one of these structures under construction deliberately avoids the question of whether it will be roofed when complete (something about which archaeologists still argue) since there is no way of resolving the issue*

BELOW *Ivan Lapper's reconstruction of the building of Stonehenge makes good use of the evidence from Bush Barrow: note the copper dagger tucked into one man's belt, the zig-zag bone mountings on the mace held by the chief figure and the gold ornament on his headband*

RIGHT *Bush Barrow, near Stonehenge. Here Peter Dunn reconstructs the ceremony in which a strongly-built man was buried with a stone macehead, carved bonework, two copper daggers, a bronze axe and spearhead, two decorated pieces of sheet gold and a gold belt-hook*

LEFT *In this 14th century reconstruction the legendary Merlin is credited with having placed the huge lintels on the uprights of Stonehenge after transporting the stones from Ireland by his magic power*

fashionable at this time in southern Britain, and something of this sort may well have preceded the more famous stone circle of Stonehenge. Indeed, it is quite possible that the Stonehenge we see today is a permanent stone-built memorial to a much older timber building whose traces have been largely obliterated but whose memory it was necessary to preserve.

Speculations like this emphasise once again the difficulty we have in moving from the 'how' to the 'why' of the prehistoric past. With Stonehenge, even the 'how' is hard enough to answer! Were the famous bluestones really brought to Wiltshire by human hands rather than by glaciers? Why go so far for raw materials? How were the even larger sarsen stones erected? Was it really such a mysterious skill, or are we underestimating the day-to-day

skills of the prehistoric craftsmen who put up the earlier wooden buildings and who now undertook to assemble a huge stone framework using familiar carpentry joints?

Even more difficult to gauge are the claims that places like Stonehenge were built as astronomical observatories, rather than as stage-sets for elaborate rituals governing the economic and social life of the community. How can we ever hope to know? Stonehenge is the most accomplished piece of prehistoric architecture in Britain, but even so it is too eroded and too altered for us to be certain about any great precision of alignment. Still less can we know whether any ceremonies held there were scientific, religious or social. Like all great buildings, it must have been designed to accommodate and enhance some predetermined pattern

of behaviour – but what that pattern was we can only guess.

Guessing, through the pen or paintbrush of the archaeological artist, is part of the fun. We can deduce something about the sequence of activity represented by the creation, use and abandonment of a tomb or a temple. A drawing or painting, however, forces us to make explicit our assumptions about matters like clothing, painting or tattooing, facial hair, body language and so on. As with the monuments of the earlier Neolithic period, we can draw on anthropological evidence, but only to a limited extent. Once again, what was most important in life is the part we know least about.

Providing we are honest about it, reconstruction drawing is one of the best ways of setting out and testing our ideas.

IRON AGE WARRIORS SETTLE BEHIND EARTH WALLS

Most of the great construction projects carried out by early farming communities in Britain aimed at providing settings for ceremonies and rituals. Our later prehistory, however, saw a greater emphasis on measures for defence.

Rising populations and a cooler climate led to increasing competition for resources. A 'them and us' attitude came to prevail as separate communities laid claim to recognisable territories, dividing up the landscape with banks and ditches stretching over many miles. Within these territories, hilltop settlements gradually took on a more martial appearance. Wooden palisades were replaced by massive ramparts topped by breastworks. Entrances, normally the weakest points in any defensive system, were gradually elaborated to a point far beyond the merely practical and related rather to tribal status and prestige. Combat, display and ceremonial feasting seem to have occupied the thoughts of the builders of these hillforts.

These people spoke a Celtic language – one of a group of related languages once spoken across much of Europe but now found mainly in Wales, Cornwall, Scotland and Ireland. It is not easy to say when this language was first introduced to these islands. The first Celtic speakers were probably non-literate: certainly, no native inscriptions or documents survive from this time. However, it is quite possible that an early form of Celtic was spoken in parts of Britain long before the Iron Age.

By the time that Roman writers provide the first descriptions of Celtic society, the southern part of Britain at least was organised into large tribal confederations, some of which struck coins proclaiming their identity. In some cases the economic and political centres of these confederations can still be identified, defended by extensive systems of defensive banks and dykes. Further to the north and west, however, where hilly terrain made communication and control more difficult, the tribal groupings may have been smaller: certainly, the defended settlements are smaller and more widely-scattered, perhaps reflecting kinship groups and clans rather than political confederations.

ABOVE *Drawing on archaeological evidence from excavations at hillforts such as Maiden Castle and on an experimental full-scale replica at Butser in Hampshire, Paul Birkbeck tries to convey the domestic atmosphere in a large single-roomed Iron Age house. In the darkness it is difficult to pick out details of any decoration*

ABOVE *The houses of the Romano-British Iron Age near Land's End in Cornwall were quite different from those of the eastern counties. At Chysauster, as Judith Dobie shows, the small rooms within the thickness of the massive stone walls may have been individually roofed, leaving the central space as an open courtyard*

ABOVE *From the evidence revealed by excavation it is not always clear which of the round 'houses' in the great Iron Age hillfort of Maiden Castle really were homes and which were barns or store-sheds*

ABOVE *The round thatched houses or sheds of the second period of occupation at Maiden Castle were found clustered together in small groups, possibly indicating the living or working areas of separate families (Miranda Schofield)*

RIGHT *Photograph of a house built by Peter Reynolds at the experimental Iron Age farm at Butser in Hampshire which has thrown new light on many previously controversial issues*

Warfare became a way of life. Ramparts were made ever higher. Defences were doubled or even trebled to slow down attackers and make them more vulnerable to the defenders' missiles. In the entrance gaps through the tumbled remains of these once-formidable barriers, archaeologists have found empty sockets which once held massive timber posts. It is still not clear whether these posts just supported fighting platforms or whether tall timber towers once rose high above the gates. What is clear is that today the gentle grassy profiles of these forts give very little idea of how imposing they once looked.

Some forts were permanently occupied by large communities, with buildings laid out fairly regularly along meandering streets. The traces of houses, sheds, granaries and storage pits have been found by excavation or detected by the less destructive process of electromagnetic or resistivity survey. Other forts seem to have been only sparsely or intermittently occupied — perhaps serving as places of refuge in time of need rather than as permanent settlements.

The houses inside these forts were small and round in plan. In the lowland areas of Britain, where timber was used, there is often only the merest shadow of the buildings left in the ground. While the sockets for the posts forming the main framework can still be seen, the walls themselves have left hardly any trace. Were those walls once decorated? Were the posts once carved or painted?

In the upland areas, the stone walls of houses sometimes survive. Even here, however, the collapse of the roofs means that frost and rain have removed any traces of internal plastering and decoration. Just what it was like to live in an Iron Age house can only be surmised. A faint echo of those times can be heard, however, in early Welsh and Irish epic literature – written down many centuries later but deriving much of its material from Iron Age Celtic societies. Other aspects of artists' reconstructions can be tested by practical experiments aimed at finding out how roofs might have been constructed, how long mud-coated walls could last in a damp climate, and how comfortable these houses might have been. Even so, most 'experiments in Iron Age living' probably tell us more about our own 20th-century prejudices than about Iron Age life!

ABOVE *Grinding corn for flour on a saddle-shaped stone quern (Judith Dobie)*

ABOVE *Grinding corn with a two-part rotary quern (Judith Dobie)*

ABOVE *Spinning woollen thread with spindle weighted with a perforated stone (Judith Dobie)*

BELOW *An upright loom for weaving cloth. The vertical warp threads are kept taut with clay weights*

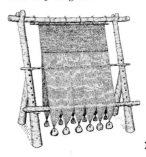

LIFE IN A HILLFORT

The best known Iron Age fort in Britain is probably Maiden Castle in Dorset. Here, more than five thousand years ago, early Neolithic farmers marked out one end of a chalk hilltop by a double chain of discontinuous ditches. Their purpose is far from clear: the area may have been enclosed for social and ritual, rather than defensive, purposes. A modern analogy might be a County Show ground, where throughout the seasons events of different size and purpose take place within an arena used by the whole community only once or twice a year.

After this enclosure was abandoned the area appears to have remained deserted, used only for the burial of the dead. Around 500 BC, however, the local Iron Age tribe enclosed the hill top with large ramparts which completely buried the Neolithic ditches. Two hundred years later the fort was doubled in extent. Additional layers of defence were then added to impress, confuse and trap the enemy. Over the centuries Maiden Castle came to symbolise the power and prestige of its occupants.

It is only from later Roman writers that we know the name of the tribe who built and used this hilltop fortress. They were the Durotriges, part of whose name survives in the word Dorset. Their hillfort was the predecessor of the Roman town of Durnovaria, known to us today as Dorchester and after two thousand years still one of the chief towns of the area.

Much of what we know of Maiden Castle comes from a series of excavations carried out in the 1930s by Dr (later Sir) Mortimer Wheeler. These captured the imagination of the public at the time, particularly on account of Wheeler's ability to conjure up in words the life and violent death of this early British stronghold. Wheeler's work has since been amplified by later excavations and by electromagnetic survey which allows us to detect the buried pattern of roads, buildings and storage pits covering the huge area enclosed within the defences. To interpret that pattern, however, we must look to another southern British hillfort – Danebury in Hampshire.

ABOVE *Roman writers noted that Celtic warriors frequently went into battle half-naked like this man from the Silures tribe in what is now south Wales. His elaborate shield marks him out as a member of the tribal aristocracy (Geraint Derbyshire)*

ABOVE *Maiden Castle was the tribal centre of the Durotriges. Defended by four successive lines of earth wall, it was occupied by them for some 500 years. Stormed by a Roman legion, it was abandoned in favour of an undefended new town called Durnovaria (Dorchester) – the New Town of the Durotriges. This reconstruction by Paul Birkbeck draws on evidence from electromagnetic survey and from excavations in the 1930s and 1980s*

ABOVE *Deep below the Iron Age ramparts of Maiden Castle excavators found the ditches of a Neolithic enclosure built 3000 years before. The exact purpose of such enclosures is still unknown (Miranda Schofield)*

ABOVE *Iron Age tribesmen armed with slings (Paul Birkbeck). Piles of rounded pebbles for use as sling-shot were found at Maiden Castle*

The excavators thought that as many as fifty of these houses might have been in use at a time, suggesting a community of around two hundred people. The huge number of storage pits, however, would seem to have had a capacity large enough to feed five times this number. In times of trouble Danebury may thus have been a place of refuge for people from the surrounding districts. On the other hand, it could have acted as a redistributive centre for a society built round the control of food and specialist materials – in other words, a town.

The word town conjures up a picture of noise, bustle, markets and commerce. It is very difficult to say to what extent Danebury and Maiden Castle were really towns in this sense. Through discussions between archaeologists and archaeological artists, however, we can arrive at drawn reconstructions that set out our tentative conclusions, offering them as subjects for further discussion and analysis.

Although Danebury is not as big as Maiden Castle, the pattern of post-sockets, roads and storage pits revealed by excavation there closely matches that detected at Maiden Castle. At Danebury we can see the traces of something which we might be tempted to call a town.

Danebury was built by the tribe of the Atrebates, the aggressive neighbours of the Durotriges. There were at least three streets running through the hillfort, lined by what seem to have been square wooden granaries raised on stilts to keep out rats and mice. Further back, at each side, rows of round thatched houses stood in the shelter of the great earth ramparts.

RIGHT *At Danebury hillfort in Hampshire excavation has revealed orderly lines of former buildings, their positions marked by recurring patterns of post-sockets. It is thought that the rectangular buildings may have served as granaries, as shown in this drawing by Karen Guffogg. It would seem that round buildings were preferred for houses, evidently as a matter of tradition rather than technology*

THE COMING OF THE ROMANS

With the Roman seizure of Britain there is a huge increase in the amount of contemporary information about people, buildings and events. Written histories, statues and inscriptions, occasional personal letters – these provide an insight altogether lacking for earlier times.

Southern Britain had already had some contact with Rome before the invasion in AD 43, partly through political alliances following Julius Caesar's two military expeditions in 55 and 54 BC, but mainly through trade with the nearby Roman province of Gaul. The powerful chieftains of the southern confederations eagerly acquired luxury items such as glass, fine table wares and wine: in return they exported gold, tin, copper, iron and slaves. It is from Caesar's own account that we gain our earliest first-hand description of the physical appearance of the southern Celts in the last century before their final subjection – their tall stature, long hair, drooping moustaches and blue body-tattoos.

The general progress of the conquest is known from adulatory histories and biographies, like the historian Tacitus's description of the campaigns of his father-in-law, Agricola. From carvings such as those on Trajan's Column in Rome, however, we can learn what Roman legionaries actually looked like on campaign. From these we can picture what the men of the Second Augusta Legion might have looked like as they advanced on Maiden Castle under their general Vespasian. We can work out how the dreaded ballista was able to put down a barrage of missiles before the final assault on the gates. We can draw in, with some confidence, the missing upper parts of timber watch-towers and barrack blocks in the forts set up within newly-conquered hillforts or at newly-established legionary bases like Caerleon and Chester.

Even so, archaeological excavations continue to provide crucial details regarding the garrisoning of Britain, the building and abandonment of forts and the accommodation offered in them to legionaries and their officers. Hospitals, stables and workshops, often passed over in official records, have all left their trace in the soil.

18

RIGHT *Under the cover of a preliminary artillery barrage, and protected by their shields from a rain of slingshot, men of the Second Augusta legion prepare to storm the ramparts of Maiden Castle. In this drawing by Paul Birkbeck the hillfort defences are shown as grass-grown slopes. It is more likely that they would have been faced with wood or cob and topped by palisades*

ABOVE *The north-western corner of the great legionary fortress at Caerleon in South Wales in the later 1st century AD, shortly after the Romans had 'pacified' the area. Excavations here uncovered traces of the first turf-and-timber defences and the regularly spaced wooden barracks shown in this drawing by John Banbury: the wooden wall-turrets have been added on the basis of evidence found at other Roman forts*

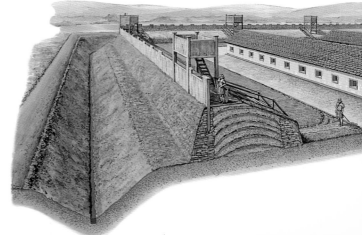

RIGHT *Within two generations the timberwork of the defences at Caerleon was replaced by a more effective stone wall with stone watch-towers set at regular intervals. The original wooden barracks were also rebuilt in stone on exactly the same layout as the old ones (John Banbury)*

BELOW *Within a wooden chest found at the military supply base at Corbridge were at least 6 sets of mititary armour, 20 spearheads and crossbow bolts, together with tools, papyrus, writing tablets and rope. The chest, drawn here by Peter Connolly, was buried about AD 120-130 for reasons still unknown*

ABOVE *From the evidence of the Corbridge hoard and the scenes carved on Trajan's Column in Rome, we can build up a fairly reliable picture of a Roman legionary soldier at the time when the Roman province of Britannia was being consolidated (Geraint Derbyshire)*

At the time of the conquest of Britain the Roman army was an extremely disciplined force, whose strength lay not just in its weaponry but also in its training. The speed with which a legion on the march could throw up a protective overnight entrenchment, for example, led one contemporary to remark that it was as though the legionaries carried a walled town in their packs!

Even were this not understood from literary sources, it would be apparent from the layout of Roman military bases as revealed by excavation. The withdrawal of the Twentieth Legion from its base in Perthshire in AD 86, for example, was a meticulous operation, planned and carried out in ways which would bring credit to any modern regiment. The barracks were swept-out before being dismantled, the sweepings being tidied into heaps at regular intervals. The timber barrack-frames were sent south to the supply depot. Even the bent and unusable iron nails were collected (10 tonnes of them) and concealed in a pit to prevent them falling into enemy hands!

RIGHT *Each legion included an artillery unit equipped with ballistae. These large mechanical crossbows fired long iron-tipped javelins. From the number of these missiles, it would appear that the defences of Iron Age hillforts were sometimes 'softened up' by an artillery barrage before the final assault (Paul Birkbeck)*

ROMAN FORTS IMPOSE CONTROL

The new Roman province of Britannia had to be rendered peaceable if it was to be profitable and pay for the policing of the new north-western frontier of the Empire.

Five years after the invasion much of the heartland of lowland Britain had been secured and a frontier established along the line of the Fosse Way from Exeter to Lincoln. This may well have been all that was intended. By AD 60, however, a dramatic change of military strategy had taken a Roman army as far as Anglesey and by AD 73 a base had been established at York. From there Agricola, in six swift campaigns, reached into the highlands of Scotland as far as the Moray Firth.

Events elsewhere in the Empire, however, required the removal of troops from Britain and in the words of Tacitus 'the conquest of Britain was completed and then let slip'. The northern frontier was withdrawn, first back to what is now central Scotland and then back further still to a line from the Solway to the Tyne. There the Emperor Hadrian established the wall which still bears his name. Although there was an attempt to reoccupy southern Scotland twenty years later, it was shortlived and the line chosen by Hadrian remained the formal limit of the Empire as long as Britain remained a Roman province.

The form of this frontier was complex: the wall itself, with fortlets and signalling turrets closely spaced along its length; a series of larger garrison forts, more widely-spaced; a road running behind the wall; and at the rear, an earthwork marking off the whole military zone. Beyond the wall's end to the west, a line of fortlets and signal towers protected the Cumbrian coast against sea-borne attack.

Almost everything we know about this vast military undertaking comes from archaeological investigation. A century of excavation has produced a wealth of detail concerning not just the construction of the wall with its forts and turrets, but also the troops who built them – the men of the Second, Sixth and Twentieth Legions. Unit by unit, they proudly left a record of their presence, carved into the stonework.

The wall was not designed to be defended against frontal attack. Rather, it was intended to channel and control movement across the frontier and to act as a linear base from which offensive and defensive sorties could be made into the lands beyond the wall. Inevitably, over the years there were a number of alterations to these arrangements as tactics changed and different military units were deployed.

Garrison duties were carried out by auxiliary troops, rather than by legionaries. We don't know which

RIGHT *During the second phase of Hadrian's Wall, forts such as Chesters in Northumberland were built astride the line of the wall. Three of the new fort's four main gates opened into the area north of the wall, allowing a rapid deployment of the garrison in case of emergencies in this frontier area. A small civilian settlement grew up under the protection of the fort to serve the garrison, as shown in this drawing by Alan Sorrell*

BELOW RIGHT *Small fortlets, now known as 'milecastles', guarded gateways through Hadrian's Wall into Caledonia. The entrance to each milecastle was protected by a tower of two or three storeys, with barrack buildings to either side. Here at Sewingshields, however, a steep cliff meant that a gateway through the wall would have served no useful purpose. Nevertheless, the Imperial authorities still provided a milecastle to preserve the regularity of the pattern (Frank Gardiner)*

particular units were assigned to this work, but their size and nature can be deduced from the accommodation provided. There were cavalry units up to 1000 strong on each flank, with mixed cavalry and infantry units of between 500 and 1000 men in each of the main forts. A further 1500 men must have been engaged in patrolling the wall itself. Overall, there were probably about 15,000 men in the frontier zone.

LEFT *The bath house just outside the defences of the fort at Chesters is one of the best preserved in Britain. This reconstruction was drawn by Alan Sorrell in the 1950s when not so much was known about this sort of building as now. Today we might suggest a less elaborate form of roofing*

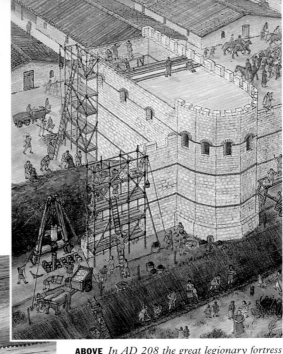

ABOVE *In AD 208 the great legionary fortress at York became the headquarters of the Emperor Severus and the base for his campaigns to regain control of the land south of the wall. The opportunity was taken to update the defences of York with large projecting wall-towers capable of mounting mechanical crossbows and catapults (Tracey Croft)*

ABOVE *The line of Hadrian's Wall was carried across the river at Chesters on a bridge. Since only the lower parts of the stone piers have been found, it is not certain what the upper parts looked like. In this drawing by Frank Gardiner the carriage-way is shown supported by stone arches, whereas in the larger drawing to the left Alan Sorrell has suggested a timber superstructure*

LEFT *Along the line of the wall, between regularly spaced milecastles, were small turrets from which messages could be passed by smoke or beacon fires. The upper parts of these turrets do not survive. One possibility is shown by Frank Gardiner in his drawing of the turret at Denton near Newcastle*

RIGHT *The signalling turret at Brunton on Hadrian's Wall east of Chesters Fort, as it might have been in the early 2nd century AD. Here Frank Gardiner has shown another form of construction, different from that shown at Denton. There is no way of knowing which reconstruction is more correct. Possibly neither is exactly right*

Alongside the garrison forts there grew up settlements for retired soldiers, traders and camp-followers. Soldiers and civilians alike dedicated altars to their gods or were commemorated by tombstones reflecting their tribal origins. Many of these people, whether officers, auxiliaries or traders, came from other lands. Regina, a Briton, was married to a man called Barates who was apparently a merchant from Palmyra in Syria: the style of the carving on her elegant tombstone suggests it may have been carved by an immigrant craftsman from that far end of the Roman Empire.

Other tombstones tell a simpler story. Regina was thirty years old when she died, but Vellibia Ertola was only four and her much less sophisticated tombstone shows this little girl clutching her favourite ball to her chest. Did her grieving parents bury the ball with her, one wonders?

Other glimpses of frontier life come from wooden writing-tablets recently found preserved in waterlogged soil in a civilian settlement beside the fort of Vindolanda. Lucius acknowledges a gift of forty oysters from a friend. Claudia Severa, apparently the wife of a fort commander, sends regards from her family to Sulpicia Lepidina and invites her to her birthday party. A soldier writes to Gratius Crispinus, asking him to have a word on his behalf with the provincial governor about his military service.

With voices like these echoing in their ears, archaeological artists can now begin to empathise more with life on Rome's northern frontier. In future we may be able to watch their architectural reconstruction drawings coming more alive with 'real' people.

LIFE IN A ROMAN CITY

Cities and towns were among the most effective instruments used by the Imperial authorities to consolidate their new province and to persuade the British of the benefits of Roman rule. Celtic aristocrats were encouraged to adopt Roman ways, to give their children a Roman education and to believe that what raised mankind above barbarism was residence in a town or city and participation in its affairs.

Towns and trading posts had existed in southern Britain before the conquest. Now, however, Britain was brought within an Empire in which self-governing towns and cities were the basis of political life. *Coloniae* of retired legionaries were planted at Colchester, Lincoln and Gloucester, and new towns were established across the province to refocus tribal loyalties and provide new local identities. Thus the Roman town of Durnovaria grew up in the shadow of the deserted hillfort of Maiden Castle, for so long the chief place of the Durotriges.

Initially the new towns were undefended. Only later did it become necessary to enclose them with walls. The all-important symbol of their status was a town hall – an enclosed market place (forum) with an adjoining council chamber and courthouse (basilica). Public affairs were controlled by a council, membership being based on a property qualification, aided by magistrates and public works officers. Although public service conferred social status, there was a price to be paid. People who were prominent in public life were expected to provide such civic amenities as fountains, statues and even entertainments in the new amphitheatres.

In addition to the new administrative centres there were other smaller and grubbier towns depending on commerce alone. However, as trade between Britain and other parts of the Empire developed, and the populations of these towns became more cosmopolitan, the buildings took on a more Mediterranean look. Where stone or brick were lacking timber was used, but always rendered over so as to simulate a more 'Roman' facade. Wealth, prestige, status and social competition: these were the forces that shaped small town life, then as now.

ABOVE *The west gate of the Roman town of Venta Silurum, now Caerwent in south Wales. At first the town was deliberately left undefended. However, by the end of the 2nd century the military situation had deteriorated and defences of earth and timber had to be added. By about AD 330 the timberwork was replaced with stone. This drawing by John Banbury shows how closely the defences of towns like Caerwent resembled those of forts like Caerleon*

RIGHT *The forum or market place of Caerwent, with the great council chamber and courthouse in the background. This complex was the seat of local government, the commercial hub of the town and the focus of public life for the Silures tribe. Excavation has provided most of the evidence which John Banbury has used in this reconstruction, but the details of windows, shutters and railings are all conjectural*

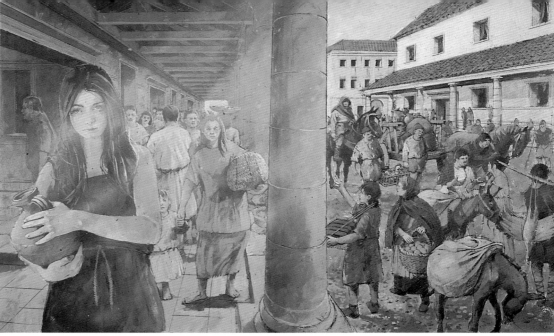

Almost nothing survives of these towns today: just an occasional fragment of wall jealously guarded amidst the bustle and noise of a modern town. Below ground, the major public buildings will have left easily identified traces, even when later generations have removed most of the stone for their own buildings. It is much more difficult to detect the outlines of mud-brick buildings which crumbled once their weather-proof coatings of plaster and limewash were no longer regularly maintained. Most difficult of all are the timber-framed houses, warehouses and shops which rested on the ground surface without the need for foundations. Only the most meticulous excavation will recover the shape of these buildings.

We must thus turn to the trowel of the archaeologist and the pen of the artist for any picture of town life at this time. Beneath modern cities like York and London, investigation is painstakingly slow: it is only after decades of work that a hazy outline of life in Roman times begins to emerge. Where the modern town occupies a different site from its Roman predecessor, as at Hereford or St Albans, the picture can be built up much more quickly. As yet, however, these towns are silent. There are no wooden writing tablets, no voices from the past, to flesh out our image of those who walked their streets.

ABOVE *Ivan Lapper's reconstruction of the forum at Wroxeter seeks to recreate something of the bustle of market life rather than to reconstruct the exact form of the buildings. Inevitably, such a 'snapshot in time' tells only a part of the story; on another day a formal procession of tribal councillors or a trade delegation would give a very different impression*

LEFT *It is particularly difficult to depict the play of light inside a building when all you have left are its foundations and part of one side wall. This reconstruction by Ivan Lapper draws on evidence from a number of Roman buildings to give an impression of the grandeur of the former exercise hall in the basilica at Wroxeter*

BELOW *The ampitheatre at Caerleon. The grandstand was timber-framed for lightness and could accommodate about 6000 people, enough for the entire legion and its official guests (Dale Evans)*

With the conquest of Britain the Roman Empire reached its western limit. It was, perhaps, an island too far. Once the initial impetus of conquest was spent, the Empire was on the defensive.

In Britain, military crises and battles between rival emperors meant that experienced troops were increasingly drawn away from the northern frontier. The result was a major barbarian incursion at the end of the 2nd century AD and another a century later. Each was followed by a period of military re-organisation in which civilian security came to depend more and more on auxiliary and irregular troops. These incursions from beyond the frontier, however swiftly beaten back, reduced civilian confidence and disrupted commercial life. The towns and country-side of Roman Britain gradually recovered but life was never quite the same again.

Archaeological evidence of this can be seen in the defences – first of earth and timber, later of stone – thrown up round the towns of Roman Britain. By the end of the 3rd century AD towns were being equipped with elaborate defensive systems copied from new military bases set up along the south-east coast to combat sea-borne raiders. Enemies were no longer just knocking at Britain's front gate: they were banging on the back door too!

Inevitably, there was a change in the character of town life. The wealthier members of the community became less and less willing to take part in local government or to shoulder its financial burdens. Instead they spent an increasing amount of their time on their country estates. More and more of the space inside the newly-walled towns was given over to gardens surrounding the houses of those of the governing class who still remained there. Recent archaeological work has shown, however, that corporate town life did continue in spite of these set-backs. The evidence for the precise nature of what went on in Britain's run-down town halls is tantalisingly fragmentary, since it is always the latest (and hence uppermost) layers of soil which have suffered the greatest disturbance. Nevertheless, it is clear that Roman Britain remained a prosperous province to the end.

The end of Roman Britain was not a sudden affair. Rather, the province slipped almost imperceptibly from Rome's grasp. Long after the remote island had ceased to be a major concern of the Empire, some aspects of life remained firmly Roman.

The concept of a 'dark age' which began as the Roman province fell back into native control is as familiar as it is misleading. It carries echoes of Sir Edward Grey's comment at the outbreak of the First World War that 'the lights are going out all over Europe'. It is an idea all too easily grasped by 20th-century historians who have seen (and sometimes regretted) the rise to independent status of countries which were once part of the British Empire.

No lights suddenly went out in 5th-century Britain. Indeed, many of the changes apparent during that century had their beginnings much earlier when Britain was still within the Empire. It was certainly an eventful time, with major movements of peoples across Britain and Europe: but the fact that we do not know or understand everything that was going on does not mean that the age was 'dark' to people who lived then.

Not surprisingly, it was during this period of change and uncertainty that a new religion first took a hold.

RIGHT *The bath house and exercise hall at the small town of Wall (known in Roman times as Letocetum) in Staffordshire. Wall was an important staging post on Watling Street, the Roman military road to north Wales. The large courtyard building beyond the exercise hall was a government hostel which provided overnight accommodation for officials and messengers travelling on Imperial business. The huge piles of logs in the yard by the bath house give some idea of the quantities of fuel needed to make sure hot baths were available on demand (Ivan Lapper)*

RIGHT *The central courtyard of the government hostel at Wall. Ivan Lapper has shown it as it might have been in the mid-2nd century AD. It seems to have been a two-storey timber-framed building with private rooms opening off corridors and balconies on three sides. It was destroyed by fire some time about AD 160-170, possibly during a rebellion against Roman rule in north Wales*

LULLINGSTONE ROMAN VILLA

The excavation of a small but luxurious villa at Lullingstone in Kent revealed evidence for Christianity in late Roman Britain. Some time about AD 360 the owners converted a suite of rooms within their house to form an ante-chamber, a vestry and a tiny chapel. The walls were redecorated with symbols of the Christian faith and with paintings of worshippers, possibly the owners themselves, although the chapel may well have served their neighbours if they too had become Christians.

ABOVE *The villa was built on sloping ground beside the River Darenth. Graham Sumner's reconstruction of the villa in AD 360 shows how the buildings rose in several tiers, overlooked by a large earlier tomb at the back.* **BELOW LEFT** *Pieces of wall-plaster show X and P, the first letters (in Greek) of Christ's name, together with alphabetical symbols representing the beginning and the end (David Neal)*

Initially Christianity was just another foreign cult requiring the total allegiance of its adherents. As such, it was deeply suspect and was banned by the Roman authorities. By about AD 208 the British church had already found its first martyr – Saint Alban.

Suddenly, however, matters changed. The Emperor Constantine made a unexpected conversion to Christianity and the banned cult became the official religion of the Empire. In AD 313 an imperial edict granted freedom of worship. The following year there were British bishops at a church council in southern Gaul.

Archaeological evidence of early Christianity in Britain is elusive. The first churches are hard to distinguish from the temples of other eastern cults. Christian altar furniture rarely survives. Only in the country houses of the aristocracy, where mosaic floors or painted wall plaster occasionally incorporate specifically Christian symbols, can we be sure of identifying early Christian congregations. Nevertheless, however fragmentary these remains may be, Christianity was one of the most enduring legacies of Roman rule in Britain.

ABOVE *One of the six Christian worshippers commemorated in the wall paintings stands with his hands outstretched in the Roman attitude of prayer (David Neal)*

LEFT *Craftsmen decorate the audience chamber and dining room. The mosaicist lays the small tesserae while his assistant cuts more from old roof tiles. Behind, the walls are plastered ready for painting (Graham Sumner)*

THE ARRIVAL OF THE ENGLISH

For all the continuity of life and institutions in some parts of Britain, in other parts the 5th century AD brought considerable change. This book is not written in Latin, the official language of the Roman Empire, or even in Celtic, which continued as the day-to-day speech of much of the island province, but in a version of a language brought to Britain at this time by strangers from beyond Rome's frontiers.

The incomers were attracted to Roman Britain by accounts of its prosperity, even during the last days of the Empire. It was not always a violent confrontation. Indeed, it is not clear whether Roman institutions and ways of life were deliberately stamped out or just allowed to wither through lack of familiarity and understanding. Town life, however, was foreign to the nature of the new settlers. Cities, paved roads and stone buildings were seen by them as 'the cunning work of giants', not as the work of men like themselves.

Over the years archaeological research has done much to illumine this period of immigration, warfare and cultural change. Excavation has revealed the imprint of the timber houses and barns of the settlers and, in some cases, even of the palaces of their rulers. In contrast to the Roman period, however, we have no drawn or carved contemporary illustrations to guide us and not much in the way of written descriptions. As a result, the archaeological artist has a much more formative role to play in portraying the beginnings of English society than in depicting Roman Britain.

A reconstruction drawing makes explicit the artist's own subjective view of the past. By their very nature, reconstructions have to go beyond the facts and archaeological artists have the same difficulty as the rest of us in erasing from their minds the images left by earlier artists and (increasingly) by film-makers. At the conscious level, their drawings may be derived from the best evidence available, but subconsciously they also reflect the inherited beliefs and cultural values of the society in which they work. However, by drawing them into the open, they offer us an opportunity to consider, compare and adjust our hitherto unstated assumptions about past societies.

LEFT *The arrival of the English. Alan Sorrel's lively reconstruction shows a war party of Anglo-Saxon raiders landing in their open boats on the Yorkshire coast near Scarborough. In the background, Roman signal towers hoist smoke beacons to pass the news to the nearest military garrison*

RIGHT *The origins of what was to become the great port of Norwich are shown in this reconstruction by Karen Guffogg of early 11th century houses found during excavations in Castle Mall. The houses have shallow storage spaces under their wooden floors in the tradition of early Saxon buildings*

It is noticeable that drawn reconstructions of this period rarely show human figures in any great detail. This is not surprising. The human figure is a powerful image. It reaches out and demands our attention, inviting us to identify with it. The way in which the artist portrays that figure can colour the way we consider a whole period of time. Do the people in the drawing look confident, well-fed, in control of their own destiny? Or do they look cowed, at the mercy of the elements or of human acts beyond their control?

Sadly, we know less about the appearance of people of this period than of the people who came before or after them. We have no indication of how they regarded themselves – no sculptures, wall-paintings, tapestries or portraits. In a period where archaeologists grope for understanding, it is understandable that artists should shy away from placing human figures in the foreground of their drawing or depicting them as the prime movers of whatever is shown. As a result, the human occupants of archaeological reconstructions of the Anglo-Saxon period are often there only to give an idea of scale: they are incidental to the scene, not the cause of it. Getting the body-language right is as crucial to the meaning of a reconstruction drawing as it is to understanding the world around us today. Getting it wrong can completely distort the message in the drawing.

LEFT *Ad Gefrin – the Anglian settlement now known as Yeavering in Northumberland. Peter Dunn's reconstruction draws on evidence from the painstaking excavations of Brian Hope-Taylor to show how it may have looked at its zenith in AD 627 during a visit by King Edwin. Soon afterwards, the settlement was deliberately destroyed by fire*

FAR LEFT *The Sutton Hoo ship burial. Shortly after AD 620, on a promontory overlooking the River Deben in Suffolk, a wooden sea-going ship 90 ft long was hauled up, filled with treasure and covered with a great mound. Peter Dunn's reconstruction shows a body laid out in the boat, though no trace of one was found when the site was excavated in 1939 and some archaeologists believe this may have been a token pagan burial for someone who had already received a Christian burial elsewhere. The identity of the person so honoured is still not clear*

CHRISTIANITY TAKES HOLD

History belongs to those who can write it and in the first centuries of independence from Roman rule it was the monks and priests of the Christian church who did the writing. Almost everything we know from written sources at this time was composed from a Christian viewpoint and carries a moralising message. Pagan gods and pagan rulers received equally short shrift!

It is hard to tell to what extent the church established during the last years of Roman Britain survived as an organised force in those northern and western parts of the country which still remained free from pagan English settlement. Where Christianity did survive, however, it was apparently vulnerable to heresy. As early as AD 429 two bishops had to be dispatched from Gaul to counter this tendency, and the isolation of British Christians in the old Roman province remained a matter of concern to the church authorities in Rome.

It was not until AD 597, however, that a mission was launched to convert the pagan English parts of the country. St Augustine and his colleagues had been advised to exploit the hierarchical structure of English society and so the first converts were kings, queens and nobles: from the outset, English Christianity was firmly associated with the sources of secular power. Moreover, wherever possible old Roman buildings were adopted as churches, especially those buildings thought to have been used as churches when Britain was still a part of the Empire. With continuity of site went continuity of belief and continuity of religious authority: that was the intended message.

In the Celtic west, on the other hand, Christianity had taken a different path, less concerned with secular affairs and more missionary in nature. For a while there were two parallel Christian traditions, one deriving largely from Iona in south-west Scotland, the other firmly linked to Gaul and Rome. When these two traditions eventually met head-on in Northumbria, it was Roman authority rather than missionary zeal that was to win the day. The keys of Heaven, after all, were thought to be held by St Peter – and St Peter was buried in Rome!

The confrontation in Northumbria may have been a struggle for power, but it was played out in terms of rite: the two parties could not even agree on which day each year they ought to commemorate Christ's death on the cross. Modern archaeologists, digging in the ground, are at a disadvantage here. They may uncover the remains of buildings but they cannot uncover faith or belief. With early Christian churches, as with Stonehenge, the defining rite often leaves no trace. The buildings were, after all, merely religious theatres consecrated to the staging of sacred drama – the Christian liturgy.

Such evidence as we have, gathered from many sources, suggests that choreographed movement, gesture, chanting and incense would all have played a crucial role in religious experience at this time. To these we may add vestments, fittings, furnishings, wall-paintings and the play of light. Very little of this survives and not much can safely be inferred as to the detail of what went on in any one church building. The size of the building itself will suggest the size of the congregation, the position of internal divisions and paving may hint at the usage, fragments of glass will show that windows were glazed, fragments of coloured plaster that the walls were painted. But that's all – and it's not much. To admit this is to admit the limits of archaeology where matters of religion are concerned. Into this world of the spirit, the archaeological artist steps with some hesitation.

Nevertheless, the attempt has to be made if a properly rounded picture of life is to be provided. Thus, while we may not always be sure which particular subjects were portrayed in wall-paintings in early churches, and our reconstructions may well be wrong, it would probably be even more wrong to show church walls as blank canvases devoid of any religious message.

ABOVE *A Saxon nobleman's residence revealed by excavation within the walls of the abandoned Roman fortress at Portchester in Hampshire. The fortress was built in the later 3rd century as part of a coastal defence system against early Saxon raiders: by the 10th century it was sheltering the descendants of those raiders. Conspicuous among the thatched wooden buildings is a stone tower: this may have been part of a private church (Peter Dunn)*

LEFT *Glastonbury Abbey was regarded as one of the oldest Christian sites in Britain – a belief actively encouraged by the later monks. The late 7th century monastery included a wooden church which was by that time already regarded as being very old and of great sanctity (Judith Dobie)*

RIGHT *Peter Dunn's drawing tries to recapture the atmosphere of a mass said in the early timber church at Lindisfarne, as it might have been in AD 650. The church (of which nothing remains) would probably have been built of oak and thatch in the Irish tradition, since the monastery on Lindisfarne was established by Bishop Aidan of Iona, an Irish foundation of great sanctity*

ABOVE *The religious art of the early church was very stylised, probably for reasons of propriety and adherence to Mediterranean models rather than from any lack of artistic skill. The illustrations in the early hand-lettered bibles are very similar to the metalwork designs found on gold shrine covers and bible cases*

BELOW *Victorian artists like William Bell Scott drew on stories of early Saxon piety for inspiration, but were often more concerned with morals than with accuracy. Here King Edgfrid is seen greeting St Cuthbert at Lindisfarne in an attempt to persuade him to leave his hermitage on the island of Inner Farne and take up the office of bishop in a mainland diocese*

RIGHT *Another drawing by Judith Dobie showing what the old wooden church at Glastonbury might have looked like. No trace of it now survives, so we cannot say which is more likely to be right. The tall carved stone pillars in the foreground are thought to have been topped with wooden crosses on special occasions*

RUTHLESS NEW INVADERS

If the depiction of human figures is one of the most difficult tasks facing an archaeological artist trying to present an unbiased glimpse of the past, the challenge becomes even greater where those figures are involved in an event which has become enshrined in the national consciousness. Every nation has at least one event round which its chosen view of itself has been shaped. Artists alter the inherited view of such events at their peril.

The year AD 1066 is one of the best-remembered dates in British history. In that year Duke William of Normandy led the last successful invasion and settlement of Britain, defeating and killing Harold Godwinsson, the last king of Saxon England. The fact that William was descended from a Danish Viking who had settled in northern France, while Harold came from a family which had risen to wealth and power in the service of another Danish Viking who had made himself king of England, is usually forgotten.

The great battle which initiated the Norman conquest was depicted within a decade or two of its taking place by a team of embroiderers, most likely in Canterbury. The result of their work still exists. Almost all the details of dress and weaponry shown on this marvellous survival have been confirmed by archaeological discoveries and great care evidently went into showing the contemporary scene as accurately as possible. The exact sequence of events, however, is less sure: this is, after all, a Norman view of what happened in that momentous year!

The embroidery sets out the Norman justification for the taking of England. According to the Norman account, the events leading to the battle were set in motion by English perfidy. The conquest is portrayed as an enterprise blessed by the Pope and, through Harold's blinding and death in battle, ultimately endorsed by God. Perhaps encouraged by this use of art to justify political ambition and aggression, later artists have felt free to use the same means to 'adjust' the balance of empathy, seeking to foster a feeling of identity with the victors or with the vanquished according to their own sympathies.

The two genuinely historical scenes

shown here are both politically inspired, and each is in a sense a 'reconstruction'. The Bayeux Tapestry shows the swiftness of the Norman cavalry in vivid contrast to the static Saxon infantry. The lower border underlines that contrast. Below the cavalry there are birds of prey: the Norman knights are like falcons, striking at their enemies. Below the reeling Saxon infantry, on the other hand, are the bodies of the slain: a warning of what is to be their fate.

Three centuries later, the 14th century vignette takes the story a stage further. Gone is the blood and death of warfare. Duke William is shown in the glory of warrior kingship. His shield and horse trappings are embroidered with the three golden leopards of Anjou, adopted since the 12th century by successive kings as the Royal Arms of England. The message is clear: whatever their origins, Saxon and Norman have become one nation.

LEFT *The Norman cavalry charges the English front line at the height of the bloody battle near Hastings in AD 1066. The moment is reconstructed in this scene from the almost contemporary Bayeux Tapestry, designed by the victorious Normans and stitched by the defeated English. The Tapestry (really an embroidery) was probably originally hung in Bayeux Cathedral on the orders of Bishop Odo, William the Conqueror's half-brother. It can still be seen in Bayeux*

It may be just as well that modern archaeological artists never tell exactly the same story when dealing with the same subject. When the subject is a political or emotive one, it is extremely helpful to be able to compare the different treatments afforded by different artists.

Occasionally, an artist may deliberately produce two versions of the same scene, designed to be displayed side by side. The message, explicit or not, is that a single reliable depiction is not possible: too much remains unknown. The two versions are then indicators of the range of possibilities. In effect, the artist is saying 'Perhaps as much as this, but maybe only as little as that: we really don't know at this stage'.

The danger here, of course, is that the two versions may later become separated. The message is then lost, and each version may gain separate credence as a balanced view.

ABOVE *Jason Askew chooses a later point in the battle than Ivan Lapper. Exhausted by hours of fighting, the two armies are almost at a standstill, the Norman cavalry using the weight of their horses to push through the English battle line. The lower viewpoint emphasises the advantage gained by fighting from horseback*

ABOVE *Ivan Lapper's dramatic reconstruction draws out the courage and confusion of hand-to-hand fighting. The equipment of the professional soldiers on both sides was much the same, as can be seen on the Bayeux Tapestry. Here the Norman infantry and dismounted knights hit the front line of the English army, drawn up in a defensive formation on a low hill so as to block an advance on London. The turning point came when Duke William used his archers to open up gaps in the English line so that the Norman knights had space to use their swords and spears. The Normans claimed that King Harold initially promised to support William's claim to the English throne but broke his word. The Bayeux Tapestry shows him struck in the eye by a Norman arrow. This may have been a biblical allusion: in the Old Testament perjurors were often blinded by God*

LEFT *A 14th century picture of William the Conqueror. The weapons and armour are those of the artist's own time. This is the Conqueror not as he was, but as men of the later Middle Ages wanted him to have been – a symbol of powerful and unchallenged kingship*

CASTLES OF THE CONQUEST

The ruins of hundreds of medieval castles are strewn across the landscapes of Britain. In their dramatic decay, they remind us of the passing of an age of feudal grandeur, an age in which destruction and death could be a way of life.

Without castles, knights could not operate effectively in hostile territory. On horseback, the mail-coated Norman knight was master of the battlefield: once dismounted, however, he was much more vulnerable. His expensively-trained horse was at risk from anyone who might seek to cut its hamstrings and so immobilise it. Some form of off-duty protection was essential.

During the years of warfare, then, castles served as campaign forts, supply bases and protective horse-corrals. In peacetime, however, they became administrative centres and the residences of a feudal nobility whose social status was still indicated by the symbols of war – sword, shield, horse and castle. These were also the symbols of power, and castles were power-houses in several senses. They reflected the power of their owners; they guaranteed the continuance of that power; and they provided platforms for the acquisition of still more power.

Investment in an impressive-looking castle was thus not just a sensible military precaution: it was also a social imperative! What mattered was not just that the owner was safe, but also that he was clearly a member of an elite group whose fortified homes showed that they exercised powers delegated from the ultimate source of all power – the king. Even cathedral closes were girded with battlemented walls and gatehouses to proclaim publicly their service to a still more powerful and unseen lord, the king of heaven.

The cost of castle building in the 11th century is difficult to estimate, but it is likely that even the smallest castle would have cost a sum equivalent to about half a million pounds at today's prices. A royal fortress would have cost at least twenty times as much. For this reason, as much as for technical reasons, the building of a castle had to be spread over a number of years. Problems with cash-flow were common even then.

LEFT *The tower of the first castle of Pickering in York-shire, built of timber on a great earth mound known as a motte: beside the mound is a lower courtyard protected by a timber wall and gatehouse. Simon Hayfield's reconstruction shows the motte with a profile similar to that still seen at Pickering today. However, the motte may once have been encased in timber to present a steeper and more effective obstacle to attack, with none of the earth infill visible at all*

RIGHT *This drawing by Ivan Lapper emphasises the logistical problems faced by castle builders. Here, at Totnes in Devon, the timber wall on top of the conquest-period motte is being replaced in the 14th century by a more durable and fireproof wall of stone. The replacement of the wall round the lower courtyard has already been completed, the new wall running up the sloping sides of the motte to meet the stone wall being constructed there*

The materials used in these displays of might and right varied according to the incomes of their owners but also reflected the roles the castles were expected to play. Stone was prestigious and durable, but it was expensive to quarry, transport and use. Timber was much cheaper and it was quicker to use. On campaign, a wooden castle might well suffice.

What did the first Norman castles really look like? In many cases all that remains are grassy slopes with no trace of any stonework. We know that even the royal castle of Windsor was originally built of timber and earth. Can we really imagine William the Conqueror, the newly-crowned king of England, living there in a fortress made from rough-hewn planks set on top of a pudding-shaped mound of raw earth? This raises an interesting question: can these early wooden castles really have looked as different from later stone keeps and gatehouses as their present remains suggest?

RIGHT *Castles built of timber were very vulnerable to attack by fire, as shown here in Terry Ball's reconstruction of an early 12th century site known as Castle Tower on the Gower peninsula in Wales. The details of the planked wall and timber-framed gatehouse are derived from an excavation carried out in the early 1960s: today only a few grassy mounds remain. If the gatehouse had been plastered and limewashed it would have been much less vulnerable to this sort of attack, or to the ravages of the weather on this exposed coastal site*

LEFT *Over a period of more than two hundred years, the wooden walls of Pickering Castle were gradually rebuilt in stone. Here Simon Hayfield shows the castle as it was in the 14th century. The old wooden tower on the motte has been replaced by a 'shell keep' containing ranges of timber buildings set against the encircling stone wall. The first structures to be rebuilt in stone were probably the old timber gate towers protecting the lower courtyards, since these were more exposed to attack by fire-arrows*

Excavation has shown that grassy ramparts are often just the slumped remains of complex engineering structures. Timber was used for the frames and wall-faces: earth was added to give the weight that was necessary to withstand battering rams. It seems that in some cases even the tall pudding-shaped mounds were once vertically sheathed in timber. In such castles none of the earth filling would have been seen. Moreover, because of its vulnerability to fire and rot, the timber itself was probably always covered over in some way, possibly by plaster.

Plastered timberwork would have looked just like stone, especially if both plaster and stone were lime-washed. It is doubtful whether a passer-by would have known what materials had actually been used. No doubt that was the intention. Given the importance attached to owning prestigious buildings, no-one would have wanted to admit that he could not afford the best materials if the fact could be hidden behind plaster and paint. Bluff could be important and even in wartime a stone-coloured wall of plastered timber might delude an enemy – at least for a while!

Early Norman castle builders probably saw no real difference between castles made of stone or timber. It is just the different way in which these materials decay and collapse that has misled us into thinking that timber castles were inherently different from stone ones. If properly maintained, plastered timbers could last for two hundred years. So far, however, only a few archaeological artists have ventured to put this new view of timber castles onto paper, and too many histories of the Norman conquest are still illustrated with drawings of crude earth forts.

FROM WOOD TO STONE

Most castles probably started off with timber defences, even if only on a temporary basis. After all, good building stone and lime for mortar were not always available close at hand. They might have to be brought to the chosen site by barge and cart from distant quarries. Even in peacetime this was a slow and laborious business. In wartime it would be impossible.

Major building projects thus had to be confined to times of peace and prosperity. An immense number of masons, scaffolders, ditch-diggers, mortar-mixers, ironsmiths, leadworkers and hodmen would have to be brought in from surrounding areas. This required careful planning. Cash-flow in particular was a serious matter and strikes over lack of prompt payment were by no means unknown in the Middle Ages. Added to this, there was the difficulty of getting lime mortar to set in cold weather. During the winter months work had to stop and any unfinished walling was temporarily covered over to protect it against frost. All this led to most building projects being spread over many years.

Where an old-fashioned castle was to be rebuilt, there were extra problems. During the reconstruction of the perimeter defences security would need to be maintained by temporary outworks. The owner would almost certainly insist on being comfortable even if he had to move into short-term accommodation while his hall and chambers were being rebuilt. Most importantly, the business of estate administration would need to continue smoothly or there would be no money to pay for it all!

Throughout it all there was a constant tension between the conflicting demands of safety, comfort and grandeur. Today the external appearance of a ruined castle may seem stark. However, the owner would have wanted it to look luxurious as well as secure. Chimneys outlined against the skyline would hint at warmth and comfort within. Nearby orchards, or a well-stocked deer park, would suggest a leisured life. Plaster, paint and banners would have added colour, directing the eyes of visitors to whatever the lord of the castle most wanted them to see.

RIGHT *Scarborough Castle stands on a headland overlooking the sea, a position of great natural strength. From the middle of the 14th century the approach to the headland was guarded by a tall stone keep within a strongly walled bailey: the walls and towers of the bailey follow the line of earlier timber defences. In the foreground of Ivan Lapper's drawing of the castle in AD 1350 is a great aisled hall built on the instructions of King John and known largely from excavation*

What he most wanted them to see was his own house. Rising high within most castles was the lord's donjon – the ultimate symbol of feudal power. These great stone towers usually survive in much better condition than the more comfortable but thinner-walled buildings which eventually replaced them. Nevertheless, the modern visitor still has to work hard to visualise lordly life inside their derelict rooms.

Walls were plastered, and either painted or hung with fabrics. Floors were covered with rush matting or with rugs. Although in the lower parts of the building small windows would have admitted only narrow shafts of light, on the upper floors the windows would have been larger. As the medieval visitor moved up through the building towards the lord's apartment light, colour and formality would all have increased.

BELOW *Stone walls could be beaten down by boulders hurled by large catapults. This drawing of a Trebuchet is based on a full-size working model at Caerphilly Castle in Wales. It can throw a boulder a distance of more than 100 yards. The author has actually fired this machine*

BELOW *The siege of Rochester Castle in AD 1215 was one of the epic engagements of the Middle Ages. Unable to take the keep by storm, King John managed to undermine one corner, causing it to collapse. 'After this', said one medieval chronicler, 'few men will put their trust in castles.' He was over-optimistic*

BELOW *The keep of Scarborough Castle. Ivan Lapper's cutaway drawing shows how medieval visitors had to climb an external stair to the main door which was thus safely out of the way of battering rams. Above the entrance lobby was the lord's private chapel. The apartment on the first floor of the keep may have been used by the lord's resident constable, since this was the least private part of the keep. The lord's own hall and private chambers were on the floors above, the additional privacy and security emphasising his social status*

ABOVE *This mid-17th century painting shows Pontefract Castle just before it was partly demolished after being captured during the Civil War. Although not really a reconstruction, the painting allows us a glimpse into a vanished past: today the castle is a ruin*

TOWERS AND HALLS

Great stone donjons might be impressive but there was a limit to the degree of comfort they could provide. While the symbolism of the Lord's Tower was never completely abandoned, by the beginning of the 13th century most lords preferred to live nearer the ground where extra buildings could be added whenever necessary. Backed up against the encircling walls, and linked together by covered alleyways, the timber-framed 'houses in the castle' provided a stage on which the increasingly complicated social rituals of courtly life could be acted out.

Linked to these 'houses' were towers built at regular intervals along the castle walls. Originally, these towers were designed to provide projecting firing positions from which archers could defend the walls, and if the castle were attacked they could still be used for this purpose. However, they also provided accommodation, either in the form of separate chambers for guests or as suites of rooms linked to make self-contained apartments.

Today, usually only the strong defensive walls and towers of the castle survive. Most of the less solidly-built residential buildings have vanished, leaving just a few traces in the form of low foundations. Where even these are absent, however, the positions of the once-imposing 'houses in the castle' can still be deduced from the remains of windows and fireplaces built into the walls against which they had stood.

The spacious lawns now found within most castle courtyards are a modern feature. Originally, these courtyards would have had an almost urban appearance. Between the closely-packed houses, cobbled surfaces were crossed by paved paths connecting the most important buildings – the great hall, the kitchen, the chapel and the Lord's chamber. Within this busy space, however, there was usually one small area of calm in the form of a garden where flowers and herbs could be grown and some relaxation found from the harsh outside world. Here lords and ladies could gather to listen to music or to hear the latest romantic epics recited by visitors from the courts of France, Italy or Germany.

LEFT *Wall towers provided defensive positions for archers, but could also be used for accommodation if provided with fireplaces, as here at Bolingbroke Castle (Phillip Corke)*

RIGHT *A vivid impression of the splendour of a visit by King Edward I is given by Terry Ball's reconstruction of dinner in the great hall of Caerphilly Castle in the late 13th century. The king's coat-of-arms is displayed on rich hangings which form a Canopy of State over the high table, while his host, the lord of Caerphilly, displays his own coat of arms above the fireplace. This is an occasion for displays of power and wealth, acted out through the rituals of hospitality and precedence*

If we are to reconstruct this inner world of castles, we must look for guidance to the highly-coloured illustrations to be found in medieval manuscripts. Here, among the scenes of carnage and death, we can find scenes of courtly love in flower-decked bowers. Alongside the conventional pictures of crusading knights besieging eastern towns are pictures of shimmering castles rising among peaceful orchards and well-tilled fields. We can even find heroic maidens, walled up in mock castles, pelting their armed 'attackers' with flowers instead of spears – the arrows of love, it would seem!

While such images may not be a very exact record of what went on at this time, they give us an extremely vivid impression of how people thought life ought to be. They show us what castle builders hoped might happen within their small enclosed worlds of halls and towers.

LEFT *Within the protective shell formed by the towered walls of Bolingbroke Castle stood the formal buildings and private residence of its lord, with comfortable accommodation ranged on two storeys. Nearest to the imposing twin-towered gatehouse was the hall where large formal assemblies could be held: from here a covered alley-way led across the courtyard to the lord's private apartments. Originally timber-framed on stone footings, none of these internal buildings survive today. However, their appearance can be reconstructed on paper, as here by Phillip Corke*

MIGHTY MASTERPIECES IN WALES

Sadly, medieval life was rarely as idyllic as the scenes depicted in manuscripts. Those scenes would have seemed particularly strange to the Welsh, whose experience of English chivalry was very different.

The centuries-long English assault on Wales came to its climax in the later 13th century. The final stage drew on all the resources of the medieval English state. King Edward I's castles in Wales mark a unique combination of motive, means and opportunity. Money, men and materials from one of the richest countries in western Europe were brought together to build fortresses of national status. Not since the early years of the Norman conquest had anything like these conditions obtained and never again would they recur in medieval Britain.

To secure the northern coast of Wales, craftsmen and labourers were recruited from all over England. The castles of Conwy and Caernarfon between them employed 2500 men. Beaumaris was a 'rush' job and for this 3500 men were required. They could be conscripted for the king's work but they had to be paid. Edward I spent enormous sums on the castles he built. In those days a knight might live comfortably on an income of £30 a year, yet Harlech Castle cost £9500, Conwy £14,000 and Caernarfon a staggering £27,000 – and even then it wasn't finished. In all, Edward must have spent about £100,000 in twenty-five years of intensive castle building in Wales. To get some idea of the present-day values, we would need to multiply these sums by at least a thousand.

In almost every case the walls and towers survive to show the prodigious defensive capability of these great fortresses. Inside, however, the more lightly-built 'houses in the castle' are ruinous and less easy to understand. Imagining their former appearance is a daunting task. Even their remains can confuse modern visitors who easily become lost in an apparently meaningless labyrinth.

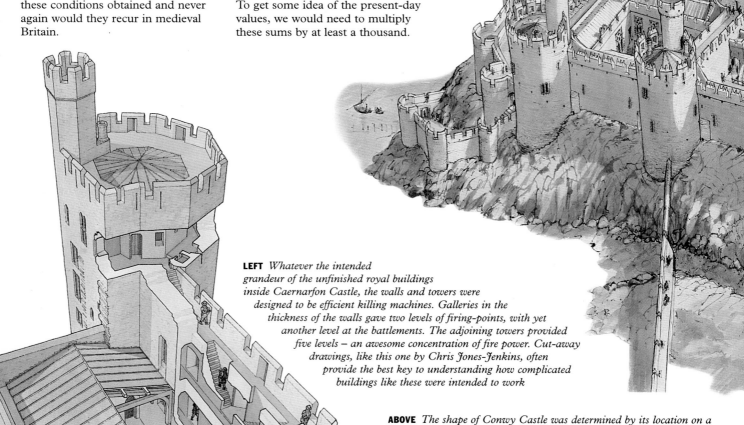

LEFT *Whatever the intended grandeur of the unfinished royal buildings inside Caernarfon Castle, the walls and towers were designed to be efficient killing machines. Galleries in the thickness of the walls gave two levels of firing-points, with yet another level at the battlements. The adjoining towers provided five levels – an awesome concentration of fire power. Cut-away drawings, like this one by Chris Jones-Jenkins, often provide the best key to understanding how complicated buildings like these were intended to work*

ABOVE *The shape of Conwy Castle was determined by its location on a narrow spine of rock. To the right, the outer courtyard housed the formal buildings of the royal administration. To the left, in the turreted inner courtyard, were apartments for King Edward and Queen Eleanor. The castle was designed by James of St George, a brilliant military architect from Savoy who was 'master of the king's works in Wales'. Even in this warlike situation there were domestic touches: within a few months of the castle being begun an esquire was being paid 3 pence to water the turf in the queen's new garden (Terry Ball)*

The archaeological artist's role is to reveal how these great fortresses were meant to function: at the most basic level, how did one get from room to room or from building to building. A reconstruction of a building on paper is less speculative, and thus much easier, than the recreation of what may have gone on inside its various rooms. The rules of stress and thrust applied in the Middle Ages as they do today, and once the structural capabilities of lime mortar, stone and timber have been grasped, the missing parts of buildings can usually be drawn in with some confidence.

When, as here, there is a need to use a drawing or painting to explain an apparent labyrinth, the artist's skill lies in being able to understand the defensive and domestic strategies which led to the construction of such complex buildings. Then, by choosing a viewpoint often inaccessible to us, and by allowing us to 'see' through the solid walls, the artist can reveal how the builders followed the designer's brief – maximising ease of movement for those who lived in these fortresses and preventing unauthorised access by others.

Armed with this modern weapon, today's visitors can penetrate the past. In their imagination, they can now follow in the steps of members of the castle garrison as they patrol the walls and towers, wait on the lord of the castle at table, or accompany his servants as they carry out their duties. Only in this way will the meaning and purpose of the labyrinth become clear.

ABOVE *Another cut-away drawing of Caernarfon Castle by Chris Jones-Jenkins. This one opens up the Eagle Tower, the symbolic strongpoint of a castle designed with a view to visual propaganda as much as to strictly military issues. The tower was intended to be the official residence of the king's regent in north Wales. The magnificence of the building, with its many large rooms, narrow passages and stairs, shows the complexity of the brief given to the king's master builder*

BELOW *The main approach to Caerphilly Castle was protected by extremely elaborate outworks, only part of which are shown here. The first drawbridge led to an outer barbican, almost a small castle in itself. From here, another drawbridge gave access to a gatehouse built on a great fortified dam which held back the waters of a lake. Beyond this (out of view) were another bridge and two more gatehouses guarding the castle itself (Chris Jones-Jenkins)*

SECURE BEHIND TOWN WALLS

Edward I's great castles at Flint, Rhuddlan, Conwy, Harlech, Caernarfon and Beaumaris were intended to be more than just military strongpoints: they were to be the springboards for the economic development of north Wales.

Edward tried every method to extend his rule over the Welsh, even resorting to propaganda where he thought it would help. At Caernarfon he incorporated architectural echoes of the old Roman imperial capital of Constantinople into the design of his new castle in order to present himself as the fulfilment of an ancient prophecy, restoring the Roman imperium after a gap of a thousand years.

Hand-in-hand with the fighting and the propaganda went the establishment of new trading communities alongside the castles. The walls and gates built to protect these new frontier towns followed the same design as those built to defend the castles.

Indeed, wherever possible the defences of castle and town were integrated in such a way as to form a single tactical unit under the direct control of the king or his military officers. Within the town walls the king's engineers laid down the framework for commercial life – a pattern of streets and market-places which still remains largely as it was set out at the end of the 13th century.

For strategic reasons, Edward's castles were sited where they could easily be supplied by sea. The long-contested hilltop castle of Degannwy, for example, was abandoned in favour of a level area down by the river's edge and there, beside the new royal castle, rose the town of Conwy. On waterfront sites like this it was possible to extend the facilities offered by the new towns to include protected harbours for shipping. Goods from the English shires flowed through the old-established ports of Bristol and Chester into the new towns where English settlers were encouraged to practise their trades. Safe within the enclosing walls and towers, foreign merchants and English royal officials jostled each other in the streets while shipmen and soldiers drank together in the taverns. Only the Welsh had no right of entry to Edward's new towns in north Wales.

Modern air travellers are used to looking down on towns and cities below them. A century ago, however, an artist's imaginary 'bird's eye view' into the past was something strange and exciting: scholarship and imagination could be combined to produce an insight otherwise quite unobtainable. Today a high vantage point is still the most effective way of setting out what we know about the topography of these medieval frontier towns and the way in which the royal engineers made use of the natural terrain to strengthen their protection.

Commercial life still continues within Edward's towns. However, although their walls, towers and gates have been carefully conserved, much of their original setting is a reconstruction – achieved in some cases by the physical deconstruction of the buildings which had grown up round them in succeeding centuries.

At Conwy, in particular, every disfigurement was systematically cleared from in front of the medieval walls so as to reveal and display them (it was claimed) in 'an ambience worthy of Britain's most outstanding example of medieval town fortification'. The result is a superb, if somewhat sanitised, view of the past as seen through the eyes of 1960s historians and archaeologists. Would we do the same today or would we be content to let Conwy tell its own story, relying on the skills of the archaeological artist to reconstruct its past for us?

Sadly, hardly anything still survives of the homes, shops or warehouses of the townsfolk of those times. Any attempt to portray the details of everyday life in the streets of these north Welsh frontier towns would involve too much guesswork to be reliable. For such details, we need to turn to better-preserved examples in other towns.

BELOW *King Edward I's new fortified town of Conwy, built at the junction of two rivers and guarded by the royal castle. To create the necessary space, and to emphasise his power, the king took over a residence of the former Princes of Gwynedd and resited a Cistercian abbey. Ivan Lapper's reconstruction draws on the surviving walls, gates and street pattern to show how Conwy might have looked in the early 14th century, a generation after its foundation*

TRADE AND COMMERCE

The establishment of settled centres of trade was nothing new in the Middle Ages. More than a thousand years earlier it had been a crucial part of Roman imperial policy in Britain. If a profit were to be had from newly-conquered provinces, it would come most readily through organised trade and established markets.

Although town life declined in the ensuing period of barbarian settlement, during the 9th and 10th centuries trade and commerce were deliberately fostered by royal patronage. By the Norman conquest there were at least 15,000 people living in London. York, Norwich, Lincoln, Ipswich and Thetford all had large populations of between 5000 and 10,000, while at least twenty other towns had populations of more than 1000 people.

The wealth of these trading communities was considerable. For the king and his earls property rents and market tolls, together with the profits from minting coins and dispensing justice, constituted an increasingly important source of income. By the early 13th century many lesser lords had also come to understand that control of a town could mean good silver pennies in their pockets. The result was a boom in new towns, with neighbouring lords competing with other to attract craftsmen and traders.

Sadly, many of these lords were unfamiliar with commerce and so were over-optimistic. Some of the new towns never fulfilled their owners' expectations, with scores of building plots lying vacant along the street frontages.

It was the huge number of specialised trades concentrated within the more successful towns that gave them their special character – and also, it must be said, their special smell! Noxious crafts like tanning might be confined to the edges of the town, but once the limits of the town had been defined by protective walls, growing populations resulted in over-crowding and unsanitary conditions. It is not surprising that it was in the great urban centres that the plague spread most quickly.

Nevertheless, towns increasingly became the power-houses of medieval life. They were the fortified 'castles' of communities of merchants bent on running their own affairs and on

LEFT *From the battlements of Totnes Castle it is possible to look down on a thriving town which still retains a pattern laid out a thousand years ago. Ivan Lapper's reconstruction strips away later medieval and modern developments to show the town as it was in the 12th century. The castle in the foreground and the riverside suburb in the background have both been added to a fortified town established long before the Norman conquest*

ABOVE *A photograph of a medieval wine-merchants's house in Southampton as restored for public display in the 1970s after being seriously damaged by bombing during World War II*

RIGHT *This reconstruction of 15th century York by E Ridsdale Tate was drawn in 1914, before scientific excavations had revealed the nature and extent of the medieval city. In the left foreground of this early essay in archaeological reconstruction is the abandoned site of William the Conqueror's first castle in York: across the river to the right is the second castle. In the background, York Minster stands in the heart of the Roman fortress of Eboracum*

ABOVE *The Southampton wine-merchant's house was built by John Fortyn at the end of the 13th century. It is one of the earliest surviving merchants' houses in England. Simon Hayfield's cut-away drawing shows the interior as it might have been in the mid-14th century, which is how the house is shown to the public today after careful restoration. The building is thus an archaeological reconstruction in three dimensions and contains further three-dimensional reconstructions in the form of replicated medieval furniture and ceramics*

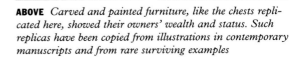

ABOVE *Carved and painted furniture, like the chests replicated here, showed their owners' wealth and status. Such replicas have been copied from illustrations in contemporary manuscripts and from rare surviving examples*

answering to the king through their own chosen representatives.

Between the two extremes represented by occupied historic buildings on the one hand, and uninhabitable ruins on the other, lies the world of 'refurbished' buildings. Stripped of their furnishings and fittings and then abandoned by their owners, such buildings have been caught in a time-warp by being refitted with real or simulated furniture and put on public display to give a more three-dimensional view of the past. In some cases these buildings are given a life after death by the presence of actors endlessly

playing out the lives of the original inhabitants.

The apparently realistic 'living worlds' that result from such presentations are reconstructions, just as much as the drawn pictures in this book. They have the great advantage, however, of allowing the viewer to step into the reconstruction and move through a recreated past. They are often more satisfying than film or theatre sets because the visitor knows that at least the walls and roof are old and that real people did once live here, long ago. On occasion, however, this apparently greater reality can pose real problems of interpretation.

In the past, as now, men and women were not particularly interested in the materials used to build their houses. They used plaster, paint and wall-hangings to conceal the differences between the various materials and allow a fashionable finish. To recreate the full effect of a medieval interior, we would need to conceal precisely those traces of the passage of time which contribute so much to a 'sense of place' and so to the special feeling of integrity which comes from this sort of reconstruction. Sense of place and accuracy can come into competition with each other.

MEDIEVAL COUNTRY LIFE

In spite of the growing interest in urban commerce and trade, in the Middle Ages most of the wealth came from the exploitation of land. Farming absorbed the labour of most of the population, even though the benefits were quickly drawn off for the support of those higher up in society. Lords acquired and disposed of estates, moving from leasing out their lands to direct demesne farming and back again as the market made it worthwhile.

Although hierarchic, this rural society was never static. Over several generations, knightly families impoverished by debt might lose all pretension to nobility. Heiresses to nothing but a name might marry the upwardly-mobile sons of enterprising peasants who had managed to buy their freedom, hold their land by rent and profit from their own efforts.

The 14th century was a time of massive changes. The Black Death of AD 1348–50 reduced the rural population by about a third in those areas where it struck. It came hard on the heels of a series of poor harvests and crop-failures that imposed great hardship on a population whose rising numbers threatened to outstrip agricultural production. No wonder it was taken to be the wrath of God for past sins.

For those who survived it, the Black Death provoked a new view of life. All the old certainties were gone. Land changed hands rapidly in a frenzy of litigation over disputed titles. Prices soared as craftsmen banded together to demand wages twice what they had formerly been. Even peasants discovered the advantages of a labour shortage.

The plague broke the bonds of society and turned the relative values of land and labour upside down. With fewer available hands to work it, the amount of land under cultivation decreased dramatically. Areas of poor soil were turned over to pasture, while lords with richer soil vied with each other to reduce rents and attract tenants.

The Black Death did not result in the widespread desertion of villages overnight, as was once thought. Some settlements were indeed abandoned as those peasants who had survived the plague seized the opportunities represented by lower rents on better land elsewhere or moved to the nearby towns. Other villages merely shrank in size, struggling on with fewer and fewer inhabitants until finally losing their viability many generations later.

There is much less contemporary evidence for peasant life than there is for life among the nobility, and what

LEFT *Much of the wealth of the countryside came from sheep. Some of the wool was made into cloth in Britain, but most of it was sold for cloth production in Flanders. Sheep rearing was not so labour intensive as agriculture, and after the Black Death many lords turned fields to pasture. A shepherd's life was always hard, and rarely as idyllic as imagined by poets and chroniclers, who were usually townsfolk (Peter Dunn)*

The commonly-held view of medieval farming as comprising three fields laid out in narrow unenclosed strips, each village with its fields constituting a separate manor, is over simple. In many parts of Britain that system never took hold. In western areas the pattern of settlement was never as nucleated as it was in midland Britain and small enclosed fields were as common there in the Middle Ages as they are now.

Even in the midland areas, where the three field system was more common, manors could vary greatly in size. On poor land several villages might be grouped to form a single manor: on richer soil a large village might be split into separate manors under different lords while still functioning as a single economic and social unit.

RIGHT *A good harvest could mean the difference between life and death since few peasants had any reserves. Food shortages often meant that the old and ill did not survive a hard winter (Peter Dunn)*

LEFT *The reason for allocating peasant ploughlands in narrow strips scattered across several fields is not clear. It may represent the sharing out of good soil or an insurance against crop failure. Whatever the reasons, the original arrangements soon became complicated through marriage and inheritance, land exchange and local dealing (Peter Dunn)*

there is looks suspiciously idealised. The seriously deteriorating climate of the 14th century is hardly reflected in medieval coloured manuscripts, where well-fed and well-clothed peasants contentedly till the sunlit fields.

Much of the evidence for medieval country life thus comes from the archaeological excavation of abandoned medieval villages. This presents a problem, however: just how typical are the remains of an abandoned village? After all, an abandoned village was clearly an economically unsuccessful village. Where, then, are we to find the remains of the more successful ones? Almost certainly they are under modern villages, and so largely inaccessible.

Where they have been found, the remains of medieval peasant houses look very insubstantial. With timber-framed houses, however, it is often the case that the better built they are, the less trace they leave in the ground, so the archaeological evidence may give us little idea of the real degree of domestic comfort they offered. Also, most of the family's goods and chattels will have been removed. Iron keys were fairly common, however: these suggest lockable wooden chests or cupboards, which in turn suggest the possession of at least some items that were worth looking after.

As with the prehistoric period, then, our picture of medieval peasant life depends heavily upon the skill of archaeological artists. In both cases, our view of the comfort or hardship of life at the time is coloured by their interpretation of what little survives in the ground.

ABOVE *Peter Dunn's reconstruction of the interior of a peasant house incorporates items frequently found in archaeological excavations: a jug, an iron key for a chest, a pricket candle-holder and a board game*

LEFT *Nine Men's Morris was a popular medieval board game. Usually only the counters survive. Here the 'board' has been carved from a block of hard chalk*

BELOW *Iron keys found during excavations show that even peasant families might have possessions worth locking up in a box or chest*

LEFT *Rush lights and tallow candles were the only illumination in most peasant houses. Metal candle-holders like this were designed to be spiked into the earth floor*

RIGHT *Dishes, bowls and containers were usually made of wood or horn. Glazed earthenware jugs were more expensive and could be used to mark the status of the family*

CHURCH FOUNDATIONS

The idea of monasticism is almost as old as Christianity itself and Britain was well provided with religious houses long before the Norman conquest. However, the introduction of Norman abbots into existing monasteries, and the foundation of new ones as the Norman barons fulfilled vows taken before setting out on their great enterprise, provided the opportunity for religious change. Almost overnight, the British church was brought into the mainstream of French and Italian practice.

All over the country abbeys and convents were rebuilt on a grander scale in the new Romanesque style to the glory of God and the new Norman hierarchy. Initially, at least, church and state were firmly aligned. Many bishops and abbots acted in the service of the King as well as the Pope.

Behind the power play, however, was a simpler and stronger ideal. Today, the concept of a monastic or conventual life may seem strange, but in the Middle Ages the communities of monks and nuns were a major driving force, both spiritually and economically, shaping the intellectual landscape as well as the physical one.

There were two main approaches to the organisation of religious life, enshrined in the separate Rules laid

ABOVE *William the Conqueror commissioned the building of an abbey at Battle in Sussex as penance for the slaughter which had secured his conquest of England. Benedictine monks were brought from Marmoutier on the River Loire to establish the new community. Work on the abbey started in AD 1070 and continued until 1094 when the church was formally dedicated. Here, the Conqueror's son William Rufus, accompanied by the Archbishop of Canterbury and the master mason, inspect stonework being carved for the nave of the church (Ivan Lapper)*

BELOW *Church and state were closely linked on the windy hilltop of Old Sarum, where the bishop's palace and cathedral church occupied a large part of the Norman town and lay in the shadow of the king's castle. Today only their foundations remain. Peter Dunn's reconstruction shows the cathedral church as it must have been at the end of the 12th century and makes good use of information drawn from better-preserved buildings elsewhere*

down by St Benedict and St Augustine. Across the centuries, however, successive reformers reinterpreted these Rules, seeking always to return to what they saw as the fundamental guiding principles of early Christianity.

As a result a series of different religious Orders came into being, each following the particular interpretation expounded by its founder, the largest being the Benedictines, Cluniacs and Cistercians. However, all the Orders shared the common purposes of withdrawal from the everyday world so as to be able to worship God and pray for the souls of the patron of their house and his descendants. All of them needed a church in which to worship, large rooms in which to eat and sleep together, smaller rooms in which to discuss community affairs, rooms in which to study or teach novices, somewhere to store and cook their food.

The great ruined complexes which we see today, grouped round peaceful cloisters, are the architectural response to these basic requirements, built to facilitate the working lives of organised religious communities living under discipline.

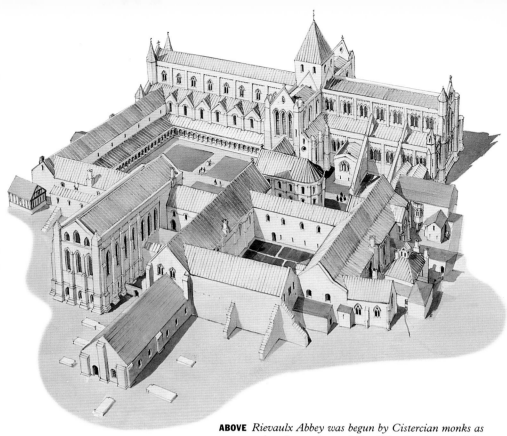

ABOVE *Rievaulx Abbey was begun by Cistercian monks as an exemplar of austerity and simplicity. By the end of the 15th century, however, it had become extremely wealthy and the rules of the community were much more relaxed. Unlike Old Sarum, much of Rievaulx still survives. Terry Ball shows the abbey buildings as they were in the later 15th century after Abbot John Barton had rebuilt his lodgings in a more sumptuous style*

POVERTY AND WEALTH IN AN ABBEY

The great religious houses of Britain acted as economic machines, converting the wealth of the countryside into prayer. Although some of their income might come from gifts of money, jewellery or plate, their real wealth came from gifts of land. It is hardly surprising that a common inn-sign was once The Three Alls: the monk who prayed for all, the knight who fought for all ... and the poor downtrodden peasant who worked for all!

It is clear that throughout much of the Middle Ages, monasteries and convents held about 15% of all the land in use. Once set up, each religious establishment was expected to be self-contained and self-sustaining. They all depended on an initial endowment of land from a wealthy patron which the community could then exploit in a number of ways. The Benedictines and Augustinians managed their land through tenancies just as lay magnates did and their senior abbots sat in the House of Lords like barons. The Cistercians preferred a highly centralised economy with their estates run by lay brothers acting under monastic discipline. Through good management and practice they were able to accept hitherto unproductive land and turn it to good account, often through the establishment of sheep runs for wool production. Whatever method was used, the basis of the whole system remained the peasant who worked for all.

Sadly, the ruined abbeys we see today give little idea of the vast farming enterprises that underpinned them. Surrounding the spiritual core represented by the church and cloister, dormitory and refectory, there must always have been a series of outer courtyards containing stables, barns, granaries, mills, bakehouses, brewhouses, kilns and workshops, orchards and fishponds. Only very rarely do any of these buildings survive: most of them were probably timber-framed rather than built of stone. In very few cases has modern archaeological excavation done anything to reveal the nature and extent of these outer courts, yet it was here that the wealth of the countryside was converted into what the community needed for its daily life, and so eventually into prayer.

Abbeys could increase their income in various ways, and one of the most profitable was the reception of guests. These included pilgrims intent on visiting the sacred (and sometimes miracle-working) relics held by many religious communities. These were usually displayed at the east end of the abbey church, behind the high altar, and this part of the church often had to be rebuilt to allow the circulation of ever-growing numbers of pilgrims without disturbing the proper business of the community – the praising of God.

Where there were pilgrims there was money. While the individual monk or nun was pledged to poverty, the community might well be wealthy and the greatness of God had to be reflected by the quality of the building in which he was worshipped. However staunchly the reformed monastic Orders might seek to set aside the wealth of the world, as time went by their churches took on the magnificence they had deplored in the churches of their predecessors.

A pilgrim entering an abbey church would probably not have seen any bare stone at all. Even the most ascetic communities plastered the walls of their churches and then painted the plaster in imitation of better quality masonry. From there it was not a great step to the inclusion of geometric or floral patterns, or even wall paintings depicting incidents from the Bible. Statues of saints were usually brightly painted. At its most extreme, the church became a theatre dedicated to the staging of the most sacred of dramas – the liturgy of the Mass. Coloured glass transformed the light within the church. Candles, incense and chanted praise combined to prepare the lay congregations who assembled in the nave for the most important moments of their lives.

Very little of this splendour survives today. However, from old drawings and prints, and from fragments of carved stone recovered from careful excavation, archaeological artists can begin to reassemble their pictures of the past. However, they will almost certainly be overcautious when it comes to colour. Our present-day sensitivities recoil from what we suspect to have been the true splendour of the medieval church.

ABOVE *The crossing and chancel apse of William the Conqueror's great penitential abbey at Battle, the high altar standing where Harold, the last Saxon king, was believed to have died. Such places were designed to express both the glory of God and the power of the new Norman king (Peter Urmston)*

RIGHT *By the early 13th century the simple early Cistercian church at Rievaulx had been hugely extended in an ostentation of carved stone, stained glass and decorated tilework in honour of St Aelred whose shrine lay behind the high altar. The unpretentious Aelred would probably have been horrified! (Peter Dunn)*

BELOW *Very little remains of the great abbey church of Byland, a Savignac foundation rebuilt at the end of the 12th century for Cistercian use. Simon Hayfield's reconstruction draws on information derived from the systematic study of fallen fragments found in excavations*

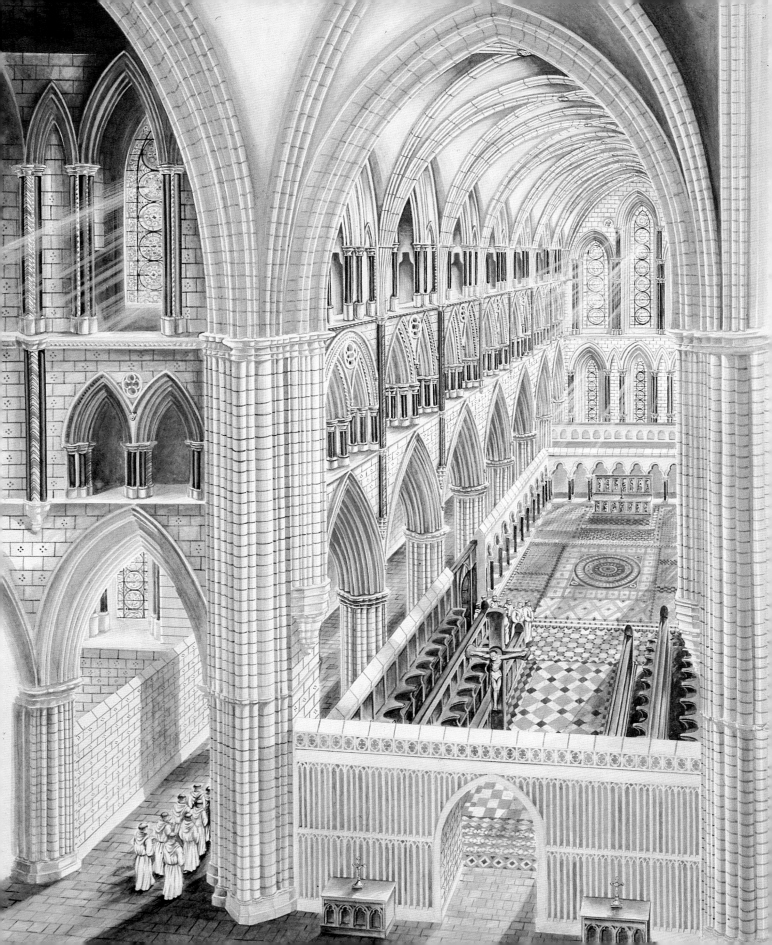

LIFE WITHIN THE CLOISTER

All religious communities followed much the same pattern of daily life. Common to all was the requirement to attend eight principal services in the church each day: round this cycle of corporate prayer the details of daily life varied from Order to Order as prescribed by their founders.

The core of an abbey was the cloister, accessible only to the monks or nuns of the Order. Its alleys linked the major buildings of the community – the church, chapter house, dormitory and refectory – and usually enclosed a lawn or a small garden.

The cloister alleys were the main workplace for study, meditation, book-copying and teaching and were equipped with wooden desks. The west alley was often used for teaching novices since this was furthest from the chapter house and dormitory and was therefore less used by the community.

Abbeys were one of the main channels through which Christian and classical learning was revived, extended and passed on. Learning was not an end in itself, however: rather it was a means of finding God. It was the non-monastic Dominican and Franciscan friars, who spent their time among urban populations, who made the greatest contribution to European theology and philosophy.

To the abbey guest-houses came young and old, rich and poor, prince and pilgrim. With them they brought news they had gathered in the course of their travels and they left bearing the news they had picked up during their stay. Pilgrims in particular were a source of international information as they journeyed to the many shrines of Christendom.

There was thus a keen, if officially discouraged, rivalry between abbeys to attract rich adherents to the cult of their particular saints or relics. It was not unknown for members of one community to make off with a prestigious relic owned by another community if they could get hold of it. Nor was it unknown for relics

ABOVE *The cloister garth at Tintern Abbey in Wales towards the end of the 13th century. This illustration shows the north alley containing the lavatorium, where the monks washed and did their laundry (Terry Ball)*

BELOW *This 'bird's eye' cut-away drawing by Chris Jones-Jenkins opens up the buildings of the abbey at Strata Florida in Wales as it was in the 15th century. Enclosed by paved walks, the cloister garden has been laid out as a herb and vegetable plot, emphasising that this too was a place of work in which beauty and tranquillity were only a means to an end*

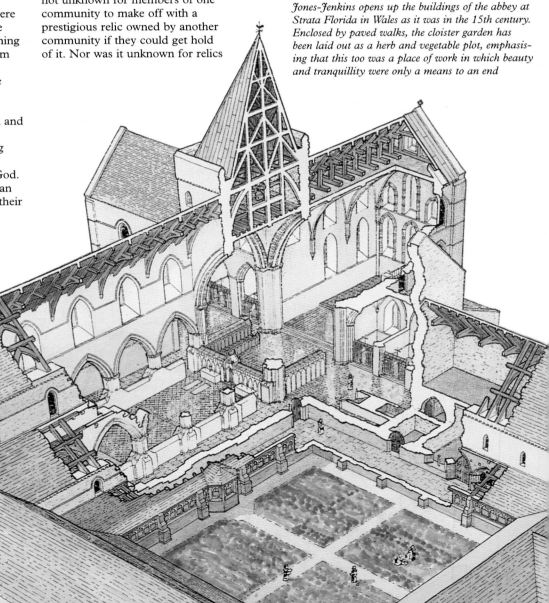

LEFT *The Divine Office was sung from wooden choir stalls set up in the central part of the church. Terry Ball's reconstruction of the ruined 13th century church of Cleeve Abbey shows (on the left) the night stairs from the monks' dormitory*

RIGHT *Judith Dobie captures a crucial moment in the economic history of Glastonbury Abbey – the discovery of the graves of King Arthur and Queen Guinivere. If it happened, the scene might have looked like this – but did it ever happen?*

RIGHT *In the 13th century William the Conqueror's abbey at Battle was rebuilt on a much larger scale in order to house 140 monks, although in practice the community rarely numbered more than 70 or so. The arcaded alley-ways of the great cloister provided an undercover exercise area as well as an airy and naturally-lit workplace for study and book production (Peter Urmston)*

ABOVE *The memories of earlier abbots or abbesses were kept alive by shrines set up in the cloister alleys, like the shrine of Abbot William at Rievaulx, drawn here by Peter Dunn. Such lavishly decorated reminders served as a daily exhortation to the community. Sadly, very few survive*

to be 'invented' if the genuine article was not available.

During the 12th century the growing interest of the Anglo-Norman court in the epics of earlier times led to a proliferation of tales about the exploits of King Arthur and his knights. The far-off headland of Tintagel in Cornwall was claimed as the place of his conception and in 1193 the monks of Glastonbury Abbey even went so far as to announce their 'discovery' of the tomb of King Arthur and Queen Guinivere. Glastonbury, with its dramatic tor rising above the Somerset marshes, was declared to be the legendary Isle of Avalon to which the mortally wounded hero had been carried to prepare for his eventual return. Understandably, the fame of the Once and Future King, as his gravestone was said to proclaim him, brought considerable wealth to the abbey.

Wealth could not save them in the long run, however, and few historic abbeys survive in anything like their original condition. For the most part they lie in ruin. Sadly, the demolition of their churches took place before historians and antiquaries thought to record them and so we must rely on evidence drawn from more fortunate survivals elsewhere to build them up again on paper. For other types of building we are better placed. Britain is rich in antiquarian records and many 18th and 19th century paintings and drawings of dilapidated cloisters survive to give us some idea of the grandeur of chapter houses, dormitories and refectories before their final slide into decay.

Early attempts to conserve these monumental complexes often lacked the skills needed to derive the greatest amount of information from their ruins. Urgent action to prevent collapse was all too frequently accompanied by insensitive ground works. Somewhat belatedly, archaeological excavation is beginning to provide details of building campaigns, alterations in lay out, the positioning of choir stalls and changes in dietary regimes, together with an insight into some of the agricultural and industrial processes that went on in the outer courtyards. At the same time, a closer attention to the details of surviving floors, walls and roofs has sharpened our understanding of the methods used by the master masons, tilers and carpenters as well as our appreciation of the logistic skills involved in the planning of these huge enterprises.

BARE RUIN'D CHOIRS

The domestic buildings of the larger abbeys usually followed much the same arrangement around the cloister. Internal discipline and external business were discussed in the chapter house, so-called from the prescribed reading of a chapter of the Rule at the beginning of each meeting of the community. This was the most important and most richly-decorated room after the church and was usually built next to it. It was customary for it to be vaulted to carry the weight of the dormitory on the first floor above: this also had to be close to the church so that the community, rising soon after midnight, could more readily attend the first service of the day.

Opposite the church, across the cloister, was the refectory. This was usually at ground level, though nuns often preferred to eat in a room on the first floor so as to emulate the 'upper room' in the biblical account of the Last Supper. Meals were eaten in silence, conversation normally being permitted only in the nearby parlour. This was generally a rather gloomy and unheated room, discouraging idle gossip. Fires were allowed only in the warming-room, and then only during the winter from November until Easter.

The west range formed a barrier between the cloister and the more public courtyards beyond. For this reason, in addition to containing cellars and store rooms, it usually housed the guest accommodation and the lodging of the president of the community who might have official business in the outside world.

Towards the end of the Middle Ages the full flood of the monastic tide began to recede. Communities began to interpret their Rules in a more relaxed fashion and in many abbeys daily life clearly became less rigorous. Careful study of their ruined remains often reveals fireplaces inserted into previously unheated buildings, traces of glazing in the old open cloister alleys and the dividing-up of dormitories into small cubicles to allow a degree of individual privacy – all the signs of much smaller communities living in much greater comfort.

Gradually, all over Europe, religious life came into disrepute.

RIGHT *The daily meeting in the Chapter House at Cleeve Abbey. The low vaulted room has a red-and-white dado with zig-zag ornament on the lower walls and the floor is paved with ceramic tiles. We now know that the stones of the vault-ribs and doorways were painted alternately white and yellow, as well as being outlined in red as shown here (Terry Ball)*

LEFT *Only the foundations and magnificent tiled floor of the original refectory remain at Cleeve Abbey. Terry Ball has made a bold attempt to reconstruct the room to its full height so as to give an impression of its former grandeur. Tables and benches lined the walls. To the right was a pulpit where extracts from religious books were read during the silent meals. The end wall may have been dominated by a painted crucifixion*

RIGHT *Like the Chapter House, the Sacristy at Cleeve seems to have been decorated in a way that only just conformed with Cistercian regulations. The rubble walls were plastered and painted to resemble square-cut stone, while the vault and basin recess were further decorated with painted scrollwork (Terry Ball)*

LEFT *The close connection of medieval church and state is shown at Westminster Abbey. Approached from the cloister through an impressive vestibule and up a flight of steps, the 13th century octagonal Chapter House is set at first floor level. As well as being the meeting room of the religious community, this elegant vaulted room was designed to serve as a Council Chamber for the adjoining royal palace of King Henry III. Terry Ball's reconstruction also strips away a range of upper lodgings (foreground) to show the vaults of the adjoining royal treasury*

People began to doubt the value of the spiritual life. Stories of immorality became common. The earthy tales written by Chaucer and Boccaccio reflected a growing cynicism among lay people. Parish priests were unpopular, too. Against church law, many were married or living openly with their mistresses and spending much of their time on private business.

In spite of this, by AD 1500 there were still more than 600 abbeys and priories in England and Wales. Many of these were under-endowed and most of them housed very reduced communities. Only one abbey had more than 60 monks and in more than three-quarters the community numbered fewer than 20 monks or nuns. Nevertheless, bishops and abbots outnumbered the secular lords of the realm in Parliament. Their political influence was widely perceived as being out of proportion to their spiritual leadership.

It was inevitable that the reaction would be political as well as spiritual. As the teachings of the Reformation swept through Britain, people of all classes began to look to the written authority of the Bible, now available in English, rather than to a distant episcopal authority in Rome. Politics and religion, never far separated in the Middle Ages, became even more entwined.

The end came suddenly. In 1533, to obtain a royal divorce and secure the succession to the throne, King Henry VIII declared himself head of the English church. Three years later his desire to reform the more lax and under-endowed communities led to the closure of almost one-third of all the abbeys and priories in his realm. Need and greed then prevailed. In 1538, following an unsuccessful religious rebellion in northern England, his commissioners began the systematic suppression of all monastic communities.

Some abbeys became cathedral churches served by non-monastic clergy. Others, stripped of their riches, were sold off to laymen who sought to profit from their acquisitions by pulling them down for the value of their lead, timber and building stone. Often the new owners built themselves comfortable houses in the former cloister ranges, retaining the outer courtyards with their barns, mills and brewhouses, together with the gardens, orchards and fishponds.

Political expediency, royal greed and the laxness of late medieval monastic life brought ruin to the great abbeys. The legacy of the change can still be seen in the beautiful empty buildings standing in some of the loveliest places in Britain, their poignancy inspiring Shakespeare's allusion to 'bare ruin'd choirs where late the sweet birds sang'. Like medieval castles, these shattered fortresses of the faith still retain their power to move the heart.

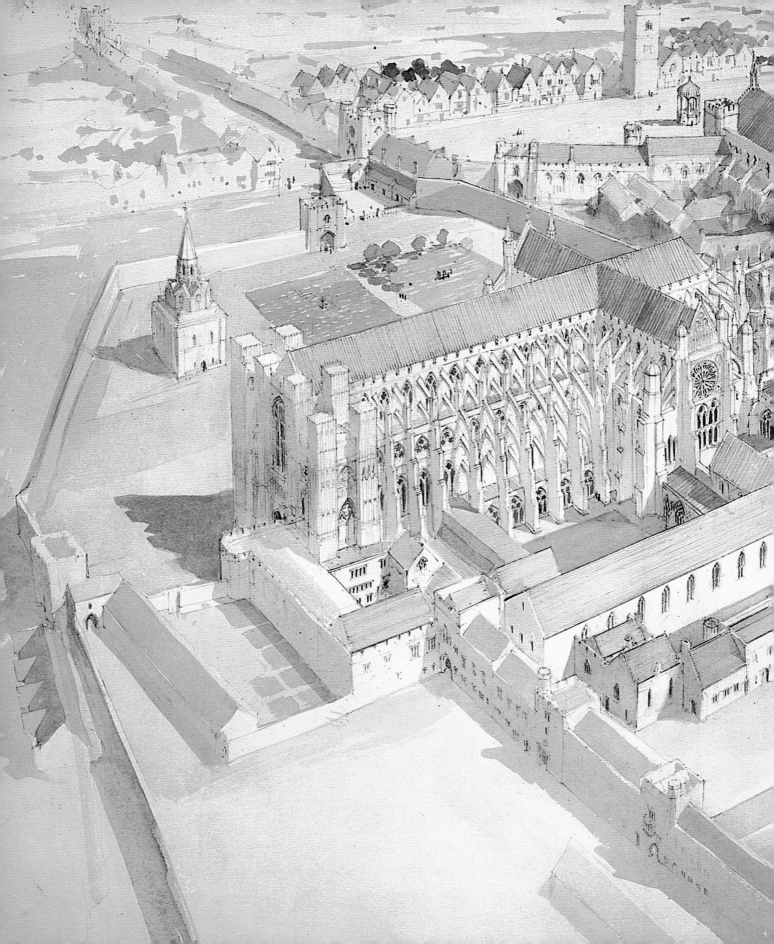

MEDIEVAL WESTMINSTER

Few places illustrate the long interwoven history of the English church and state more clearly than Westminster.

The old Saxon church on Thorney Island was known as the West Minster to distinguish it from the even older East Minster – the cathedral church of St Paul in the city of London. Beside it, successive Saxon and Norman kings built and enhanced a royal palace fronting onto the river Thames. Thereafter palace and abbey jostled together on this small island of firm ground in the marshes upstream from London and its growing suburbs.

The abbey church, chapter house and cloister can still be seen today. However, while kings and queens lie buried in the abbey, very little remains of the medieval royal palace. Most of it was destroyed by fire in 1834. A few buildings survive, hidden beneath later casings of stone and brick: the crypt of St Mary Undercroft, the cloisters of St Stephen's chapel and the Jewel Tower. However, only the Great Hall, built for William Rufus in the 1090s and re-roofed three centuries later for Richard II, remains in anything like its medieval form to show the grandeur of this former royal residence,

Extending out over the former marshland, back up the hill towards Trafalgar Square, is a later landscape of government and empire. Of the adjoining royal palace of Whitehall, from which this famous street takes its name, only the Banqueting House built for Charles I and the Horseguards built for Charles II remain. It is still the 900-year-old royal and ecclesiastical complex on Thorney Island that draws the biggest crowds.

To create this panoramic impression of what Westminster may have looked like towards the end of the medieval period, Terry Ball has drawn on evidence provided by archaeological excavations, medieval manuscripts, early maps and 18th century topographical drawings and descriptions. The result is a truly remarkable piece of reconstruction art, one of the finest of its kind.

THE BATTLE OF FLODDEN

In August 1513, at the instigation of the king of France, the largest and best-equipped Scottish army ever to invade England crossed the border near Coldstream. The English king, Henry VIII, had invaded France earlier that summer and the Scots aimed to open up a diversionary 'second front', forcing the English to draw troops away from France to counter this threat from the north.

A month later, almost a third of the Scottish army lay dead on a hillside in Northumberland. They had been defeated by an army half their size, all drawn from the English northern and midland counties. No troops had been diverted from the war in France.

The Scots, under King James IV, numbered around 40,000 men. About half were the trained and well-equipped retainers of the nobility and gentry. Another third, not so well trained or equipped, were unpaid levies from the lowland towns and shires. The remainder were Highland clansmen. The main weapon was the long pike, a continental innovation designed to enable infantry to withstand cavalry but of limited use against other infantry, as Flodden was to prove.

The English army numbered about 26,000 men, mainly the indentured retainers of the midlands aristocracy. They were not as well armoured as the Scots. Crucially, however, they were more used to their main weapons – the billhook and the longbow.

The Scottish king had drawn up his army on the crest of a hill, challenging the English to attack up the slope. When the English army came within range of the waiting Scottish cannon King James, in a misplaced burst of confidence or chivalry, forbore to open fire. When eventually he did, it was too late. His heavy guns could not be aimed down hill and from the lower ground the lighter English cannon created havoc amongst the Scots.

Stung into an ill-conceived advance downhill across marshy ground, the huge columns of Scottish pikemen lost cohesion and impetus. At close quarters the short English billhooks were deadly. The English lost 1,700 men, the Scots 15,000.

ABOVE *Dressed in the most modern German-made armour, this Scottish Earl will fight on foot with his retainers. Standing at the front of a column of newly-trained pikemen, he will lead them against the English line (Ivan Lapper)*

The Scottish dead included King James himself, an archbishop and a bishop, 19 barons, the Provost of Edinburgh and over 300 knights and lairds. In the course of three hours Scotland had lost most of her nobility, gentry and administrative class.

The details of the battle are known from the personal accounts of survivors and from military and political despatches of the time. Most of the commanders are known by name and many individual acts of courage are recorded. From these sources, and from surviving armour and weaponry, the archaeological artist can go to work. However, national pride and personal fear cannot be depicted. The noise, dust, sweat and blood of that combat must be provided by the imagination of the viewer.

TOP *Led by their king and accompanied by the royal siege-train and baggage wagons, the Scottish army marches to attack Norham Castle at the start of their campaign. Some 60,000 in number, they have with them 17 heavy guns hauled by teams of oxen under the command of the king's master gunner, Robin Borthwick. They also have 1000 hand guns and 6000 pikes, all sent from France. By the time they reach Flodden a month later, desertion and plague will have reduced their numbers by a third but they will still be a well-equipped and well-fed army (Ivan Lapper)*

ABOVE *King James had hoped to draw the English army into an attack on his well-prepared position on top of a hill near Flodden, where his heavy cannon have been set up. Instead, the English have swung northwards and have outflanked him: tired and hungry from their long march, they are now advancing towards him from a different direction. King James wheels his army, moving his guns as best he can to meet this new threat. Gathering the aristocracy of Scotland around the royal standard, he prepares to begin the battle (Ivan Lapper)*

LEFT *The 18-foot long pikes carried by the main body of Scots are effective weapons provided they can be used in close defensive formation. They can also be used to break an enemy's ranks, the diamond-shaped columns moving like giant hedgehogs. Close-packed in this way, however, the pikemen will be an easy target for the English archers and gunners. If the columns lose momentum, or break up when crossing rough ground, the pikes will not be as effective in hand-to-hand combat as the 8-foot English billhooks (Ivan Lapper)*

RIGHT *The English army contained around 1200 soldiers from the fleet, brought by the Lord Admiral. Equipped with up-to-date body armour, though with their lower legs exposed, these men provided a vital core of professional fighters (Ivan Lapper)*

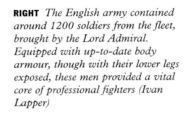

ABOVE *The main body of the Scots, led by King James IV himself, attacks downhill towards the English centre commanded by the Lord Admiral. The English left flank has already collapsed under the onslaught of Scots borderers and highlanders: there is a real danger of a complete rout. However, in crossing marshy ground the Scots formation has lost much of its striking power and the English stand firm for two long hours of desperate fighting (Ivan Lapper)*

RIGHT *The fighting at Flodden did not start until late in the afternoon. By nightfall, the dead lay most thickly around a small stream issuing from the marshy ground which had proved the undoing of the Scottish pike columns. Here the Scots and English had fought longest and hardest and it was here that King James was killed, one hand hacked off, an arrow through his jaw, his throat cut by a billhook. It is probable that the stream did indeed for a while 'run red with blood', as claimed at the time (Ivan Lapper)*

TUDOR PAGEANTRY

Our understanding of the 16th century is largely conditioned by the deliberate image-building of the Tudor dynasty.

The founder of the dynasty, Henry VII, sought an image which would transcend the preceding decades of corruption and establish his line against all challenge. Presenting himself as the child destined by prophecy to restore the sovereignty of the ancient British race, he even named his first son after the legendary King Arthur to enhance his claim of renewing the chivalric glories of the past.

More secure on the English throne, his second son Henry VIII sought a larger role on the European stage which enabled him to obtain first his endorsement by the Papacy as 'defender of the faith' and then the freedom of his realm from all Papal claims to secular overlordship or spiritual jurisdiction.

Of all the Tudors, the greatest image-maker was undoubtedly Henry VIII's daughter, Elizabeth I. Precluded by law from being both wife and monarch, she drew on the medieval rituals of courtly love to build a role as the Virgin Queen, endlessly sought-after by noble lovers but for ever un-attainable. Under Elizabeth, England's growing sense of national identity became completely bound up with the image of the Sovereign's majesty.

This required constant attention to detail. Every gesture was calculated. Every action was carefully rehearsed. The royal court became a brightly-lit stage on which successive Tudor kings and queens directed, cast and acted out the drama of their power.

A devastating fire in the royal palace at Sheen in 1497 gave Henry VII an early opportunity to refurbish his stage. His new palace of Richmond was designed to be a 'lantern spectacle and exemplar' for all the world. A similar desire is reflected in the name of Henry VIII's 'Nonsuch Palace'. Attempts by courtiers to emulate the royal buildings could lead to trouble: Cardinal Wolsey found it politic to 'give' his new house at Hampton Court to the king, who then enlarged and embellished it beyond measure.

To be seen, a sovereign needed to travel. Medieval kings had made use of the comfortable accommodation to be found in some of the monastic houses, but Henry VIII's action in suppressing the monasteries left his daughter Elizabeth seriously short of royal residences in some parts of her realm.

To overcome this difficulty, and to play one man off against another, Elizabeth frequently stayed at the houses of the rich aristocrats who served and advised her. These men had followed the lead of the court in matters of architecture and decor, in some cases almost beggaring themselves in their rivalry with their peers. Possession of a Queens's Chamber became something of a status symbol, even for those whom the queen was very unlikely to visit!

If the queen did come, the cost could be enormous. There would need to be music, masques, allegorical plays and pageants. Many of her courtiers came to fear Elizabeth's great progresses about the country.

Notwithstanding the cost, the houses of the Tudor nobility and gentry were designed for display. As the sovereign gradually changed from being a feudal lord to a more remote head of state, new and elaborate social rituals had to be devised to demonstrate and cement the structure of society, and these rituals required appropriate backdrops for their staging. The houses of the rich were at one and the same time political institutions, cultural centres and the market places for patronage.

The 16th century saw a breakthrough in the art of portraiture.

RIGHT *By the end of the 16th century most great houses in England and Wales boasted a Long Gallery on the top floor. Usually these galleries served as indoor exercise areas where the owners and their families could walk up and down if bad weather or ill health prevented outdoor pursuits. These lavishly decorated rooms could also provide the setting for special social gatherings. Here Ivan Lapper depicts such a gathering in the long gallery added to the 15th century castle at Raglan*

BELOW *At Berry Pomeroy in Devon, the rising fortunes of the Seymour family resulted in a rebuilding of the main accommodation in a style which took account of the latest French models. Very little survives of the upper parts of the building, but Terry Ball's reconstruction shows how it was intended to work. The new wing projected well beyond the curtain wall of the old castle and provided a suite of grand reception rooms on the first floor, served by a new kitchen block. On the top floor a long gallery ran the full length of the building, with magnificent views out over the countryside*

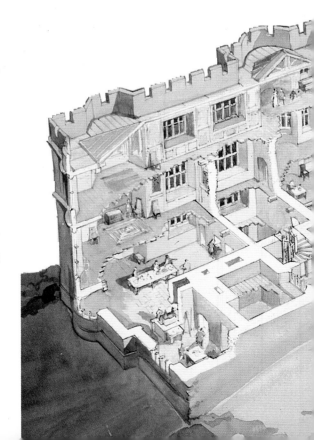

RIGHT *Queen Elizabeth I visited Lord Robert Dudley's castle of Kenilworth a number of times, most famously in 1575. On that occasion the royal party was welcomed with nineteen days of pageantry, fireworks and feasting. Here Ivan Lapper seeks to capture the excitement and splendour of Elizabeth's arrival*

LEFT *The size of the queen's entourage meant that all the resources her host could command had to be pressed into service. Food was a major form of display and lords ordered their kitchen staff to devise new recipes and wondrous confections (Ivan Lapper)*

From contemporary paintings and drawings, in spite of all the image projection, we can begin to see something of the personalities of Tudor people. With increased literacy, more contemporary descriptions of court and country life have come down to us. Many of the great houses survive in something like their original state, rather than as haunting ruins. We can sit in the chairs and eat off the tables used by men and women of that time.

With so much evidence available to us, there might seem less for the archaeological artist to do. It is no coincidence that so many 'living history' re-enactments deal with Tudor times: it is the first historical period for which sufficient evidence exists to allow such three-dimensional reconstructions, involving as they do the interplay of architecture, costume, food, music, and social relationships defined by posture and body language.

The archaeological artist still has a crucial role to play, however, in applying new perspectives to the painted scenes of courtly life, softening the rigour of the official portraits and opening up those places and those parts of society which the Tudor artists never reached.

LEFT *Pendennis in Cornwall saw the last siege of the Civil War. Modernised in 1598-9, it was better able to resist attack than many medieval castles. After five months of resistance, the garrison was allowed to march out with full military honours – colours flying, drums beating and trumpets sounding (Alan Sorrell)*

RIGHT *Starved out! Under the command of the castle governor, Sir Jordan Crosland, the royalist garrison of Helmsley Castle also marches out with honour, carrying its weapons (Judith Dobie)*

The Civil War of 1640–8 divided friends and families in a way that earlier wars had never done. The issue of contention was a stark one: should the king be accountable to his people through Parliament or only to God?

At first a negotiated settlement seemed possible. Behind the political issue there was a heady mix of social resentments, competing economic interests and conflicting religious beliefs. The early skirmishes were therefore fought by ever-shifting allegiances of people whose friendships frequently transgressed the simple divide between King and Parliament. Very few of the combatants envisaged the eventual execution of their king.

'I detest this war without an enemy' declared the Parliamentarian General Sir William Waller to his Royalist opponent Sir Ralph Hopton, an old friend and former companion-in-arms. 'My affections to you are so unchangeable that hostility itself cannot violate my friendship.... We are both upon the stage and must act those parts that are assigned us in this tragedy. Let us do it in a way of honour and without personal animosities.'

It was not to be. As the war dragged on fathers, sons, uncles and cousins found themselves opposed on issues that became more and more radically defined. The more intransigent King Charles I became, the more puritanism and parliamentary republicanism became inextricably joined in opposition to him. Hope

came with a short truce in 1646 but when fighting broke out again the following year it was clear to everyone that if Parliament won there would be no room for a king!

After the execution of the king in 1649 many of the Royalist strongholds were deliberately rendered indefensible. Battlements were toppled and gunpowder was used to break up the more resistant keeps and gatehouses. Many of Britain's most famous castles owe their present

BELOW *Excavations in the ditch of Montgomery Castle revealed over 600 fragments of obsolete 16th century armour, dumped there after the Battle of Montgomery in 1644 (Geraint Derbyshire)*

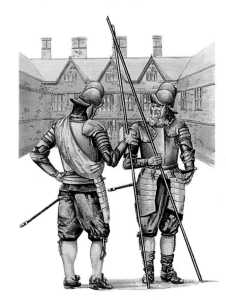

dramatic profiles to this policy. Time and nature have now hidden the scars of war, turning the shattered buildings into picturesque ruins and concealing the evidence of violent conflict. Sadly, however, the Civil War's complex pattern of political opposition, local allegiances and religious antagonisms still finds an echo in many places today.

Indeed, if there is a single theme which emerges from the study of history, it is that people in the past were very much like us now. The clothes they wore, the things they used, the buildings they lived in, may all have been different but it is tempting to believe that we would probably not find the people themselves all that strange were we able to meet them.

This conclusion may also be true for the period before history, and in this book the drawings of at least one artist incorporate the faces of famous modern people, slightly altered so that they are not immediately recognisable but seem comfortingly familiar. The use of such a subtle technique to illustrate a personal belief is not without its dangers, of course: a similarity of facial expression could mask a very different cast of mind and our view of our place in the universe may be very different from that of prehistoric man.

Nevertheless, it is clear that it is not enough just to say 'That was long ago and people were different then' in order to explain the puzzles of the past. Some greater effort is needed.

Archaeologists seek to recapture the forgotten and unrecorded parts of our history and to reach back beyond it. Artists enable them to show what they see in their mind's eye, producing what might be called 'a picture of probability'.

There are other ways of conveying this. Holograms, the rebuilding of ruins and the construction of full-size replicas, historical re-enactments, the virtual reality of computer simulations – these can all serve to make explicit our inner assumptions about the past.

Reconstruction drawings have one disadvantage as a medium of communication. They open up a one-sided conversation. Whatever ideas they may put in train must be followed up elsewhere. Nevertheless, the speed with which drawings can be made and remade, the low level of cost involved and the degree of control that is possible over their use (or misuse) mean that the work of the reconstruction artist is likely to remain one of the most powerful ways of presenting the past for many years to come.

PICTURING THE PAST

Archaeological artists work in different ways to achieve their ends, but in almost every case work starts and ends with a dialogue. Initially, the dialogue is between the artist and a group of specialist researchers. At the end, the dialogue – a silent one – is between the artist and the public.

The common aim of all archaeological artists is to open up their subject, making the best guess they can without pretending that it is more reliable or more exhaustive than it really is. The artwork brought together in this book has been chosen to illustrate this approach.

In agreeing to present the past in this way, each artist acts as the spokesman for the group whose combined knowledge went into the final portrayal of the subject. Some artists like to work from a very detailed brief: others prefer to engage in open discussion so that fresh ideas are generated by interaction between specialists from different research disciplines. Either way, reconstructing the past on paper is a very collaborative venture.

All reconstruction involves some degree of guesswork. Just how much guesswork is involved depends on the period and subject matter. Clearly, for the very remote past, almost every part of the picture is some form of guess since hardly anything actually survives from that time and what does survive is sometimes not very informative.

The increase in the availability of factual evidence from early times until today is not steady. Thus the incorporation of Britain within the Roman empire is marked by a quantum leap in the number of strands of evidence available to archaeologists and historians, but the withdrawal of Roman interest in the province plunges them (and us) back into a past that is almost, though not quite, prehistoric. Throughout, certain types of activity are well recorded or well evidenced by surviving remains, but others are not: inevitably, at all periods, the lives of the poor are always harder to reconstruct than the lives of the aristocracy. What matters is that we are honest about what we are trying to do and how we do it.

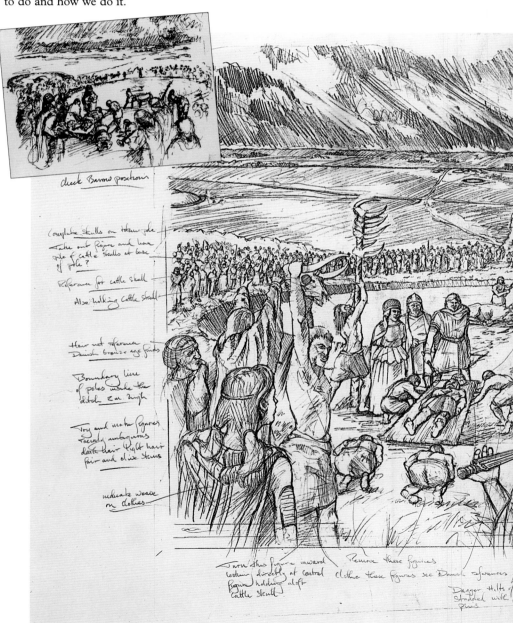